ORCHIDS

**By the Editors of Sunset Books
and Sunset Magazine**

Epidendrum prismatocarpum; see pages 32–37.

Sunset Publishing Corporation ■ Menlo Park, California

Foreword

For too many years the public image of orchids has been that of supremely beautiful flowers produced from plants that require highly specialized and costly growing arrangements to survive, let alone to grow well. While casting a rather fascinating aura of mystery over these plants, this image did them a great disservice—denying their beauty to the many people who would have liked to try growing orchids but assumed they lacked the proper skills and equipment.

In this book we have sought to dispel this mystery and thereby open the door to the beautiful world of orchids so that you can include the enjoyment of their varied charms in your daily living. Whether your goal is to have them indoors at windows, outdoors for patio decoration, in the greenhouse, or as corsages and cut flowers, there are orchids that will give you great satisfaction for only a small outlay of care.

We wish to extend special thanks to the American Orchid Society, Armacost & Royston Orchids, Inc., Philip Edinger, Ewing Orchids, Hausermann's Orchids, Inc., Frank Fordyce and Bob Johnson at Rod McLellan's Orchids, Joe Seals, Mrs. Henry J. Severin, and Shaffer's Tropical Gardens, Inc. for all their assistance and advice.

Above: *Odontoglossum* Cannero 'Pacifica'; see page 48–53.
Below: *Phalaenopsis* Tyler Carlson 'Helen Dickson'; see pages 40–45.

Supervising Editor: Kathryn L. Arthurs
Research and Text: Jack Kramer

Design: Terrence Meagher
Artwork: Joe Seals
Cover: We show two very different varieties of *Phalaenopsis: Phalaenopsis* Eva Lou (left) is familiar type of orchid; *P.* Golden Pride (*P. amboinensis* x *P. fasciata*) (right) is a newer novelty hybrid. Photographed by Beauford B. Fisher.

Editor, Sunset Books: Elizabeth L. Hogan

Eleventh printing May 1992

Contents

Special features

The Aristocrats of Flowers

. . . royal family with a fascinating background

THOSE colorful, enticing orchids that look so beautiful in corsages from the florist are not only to be admired on special occasions. The familiar gift orchids and many, many more can be easily grown at home without special equipment or elaborate care. Because of improvements in cultural and propagating techniques, they are no longer expensive; a mature plant with four or five flowers may cost less than ten dollars; younger and smaller plants will be much less.

While the most familiar orchids (the usual corsage types) are cattleya, cymbidium, and paphiopedilum species and hybrids, there are also numberless intriguing and attractive species from all parts of the world from which to choose to decorate your home. You will find orchid flowers in all colors except true black, the predominant shades being lavender, pink, rose, red, yellow, and white. Frequently two or more colors, often contrasting, will appear in a single flower.

Orchid blossoms range from nearly pinhead size to flamboyant kinds as large as salad plates, many of them providing delightful fragrance in addition to rare beauty. Flowering seasons vary enough so that by selecting according to season of bloom you can have color indoors all year from perhaps only a dozen plants.

History and folklore

Although the cultivation of orchids has been a relatively recent undertaking, the knowledge and folklore of these plants trace back many centuries to the Orient and to ancient Greece. Confucius mentioned orchids as being flowers of great refinement to be held in high esteem, and it was the Greek philosopher Theophrastus, in the era of Plato and Aristotle, who first called them by the name *orchis* from which the word "orchid" is derived. From Grecian times through approximately the eighteenth century, the native European orchids constituted a part of the herbalists' bag of remedies. The orchid root supposedly was an aphrodisiac—useful, too, in obtaining a child of whichever sex one desired.

It remained, however, for the plant explorers of the late 1700s to spark an interest in growing orchids purely for ornamental purposes. Expeditions into tropical areas of Mexico, Central America, and South America revealed much new material for plantsmen throughout the world.

Where orchids are found

Popular opinion—abetted by romanticized stories of tropical adventure—has placed most orchids as growing naturally in oppressively hot, steaming jungles. A more realistic look at the orchid family will reveal that a number of species flourish in the warm temperate regions throughout the world. A

Group portrait of popular orchids includes cattleyas (left), phalaenopsis (upper right), odontoglossum (center), paphiopedilums and miltonia (lower right).

Four orchids with diverse shapes are shown here: laelia (upper right), odontoglossum (upper left), miltonia (lower right), and paphiopedilum.

Thick clusters of white dendrobiums droop gracefully from tree fern trunks in this junglelike setting. In mild winter areas, you can create a similar setting.

few representatives can be found even in such unexpected places as frigid mountain areas or in deserts, or in streams as near-aquatics. Pleione species, for example, often break through snow to flower, while a few rare Australian species are actually subterranean—only barely reaching the soil surface at flowering time. The west coast of South America—Chile, Peru, Ecuador, and Colombia—harbors a wealth of native orchids. There they are found in quite mountainous territory where at 6,000 feet above sea level the nighttime temperature average is around 48°.

Perhaps the greatest number of orchid species is found in New Guinea, but Asia, Africa, Borneo, and Central America also have vast regions populated with orchids. Ironically, although Hawaii abounds with orchids, only three insignificant kinds are native; all the showy sorts have been planted there by man.

From jungle to greenhouse

While it is true that tropical climates are generally mild and humid, there still exist, within the tropics, sharp distinctions between *how* mild and *how* humid. Plants taken from mountainous regions may be accustomed to definite seasonal fluctuations in rainfall and temperature and to somewhat lower temperatures generally than are plants that grow in lowlands or along rivers. Even though the traveler to the tropics may consider the entire area "hot," the plant species there have distributed themselves according to these various nuances of heat and moisture.

Therefore, to know that an orchid comes from

Costa Rica is of little value in trying to duplicate native conditions in the greenhouse. To know that an orchid is found along watercourses in the lowlands is considerably more helpful, yet even within a given location the orchids that grow in treetops will prefer more light, better air circulation, and lower humidity than will those that grow close to the jungle floor.

Early orchid growers erred on the side of generalization, assuming all native habitats to be hot and steaming. As a result, collected orchid plants, upon reaching European growers, were subjected to artificial greenhouse climates which were more likely to assure their failure rather than success.

Of little help to growers who were trying to solve the "mysteries" of orchid culture were some of the plant explorers and collectors. Because it was the explorer-collector who was able to supply growers with orchid plants from the tropics, collectors who had found especially desirable species often realized the advantage in keeping the location of those plants secret, even to the point of falsifying information to deliberately lead other explorers astray. By so doing, the individual collector could ask high prices for his fine plants because they were an exclusive offering.

Inasmuch as successful orchid culture was achieved only after years of trial and error, many growers found themselves reluctant to divulge *their* secrets lest other growers, both amateur and professional, find orchid growing so easy as to destroy a commercial advantage.

Born from avarice and ignorance, the myth of "difficult" orchids persisted into the twentieth century.

What Is an Orchid?

. . . a large, diverse, and exotic plant family

T HE 25,000 or so species of orchids make up an exceedingly varied family. Many orchids are so different in appearance that it's hard to believe they are related. Even with this amazing variety of sizes, shapes, and proportions of parts, orchids do have a number of mutual characteristics—characteristics that distinguish them from other plants.

Growth habits

Many of the tropical orchids discovered and collected in the eighteenth and nineteenth centuries were found growing on the trunks or branches of trees. This growth situation spawned the erroneous but persistent belief that orchids were parasites. Actually these plants utilize the trees only for support, receiving their nutrients from whatever the rain washes their way, as well as from bird droppings and from organic debris that may collect around their roots. Such plants are called epiphytes.

For convenience, orchids may be considered to be of two basic growth habits: epiphytic (those that grow on trunks or branches of trees—just explained) or terrestrial. The terrestrial species grow with their roots in soil.

Variations on this general theme do occur. There are also orchids that cling to rocks for a foothold; these are generally treated as epiphytes since they usually depend upon natural forces to carry nutrients to them. Some species cannot be absolutely classed as either epiphytic or terrestrial. There are those that begin life growing in soil but become vinelike and cling to tree trunks or other convenient supports; then in later life the soil-rooted part dies away, leaving the plant a true epiphyte. You will also find some species growing equally well in trees and in the soil below, where pieces of aerial plants have fallen and taken root.

It is important to know the basic growth habits of the orchids in your possession, for their needs differ correspondingly. Most terrestrials need

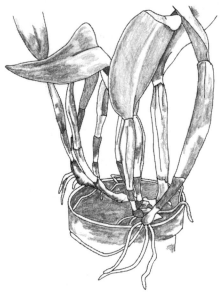

Sympodial growth *is typical of the majority of orchids. New growth originates from base of previous year's growth; it matures in one season, producing flowers then more new growth. Cattleyas and dendrobiums have sympodial growth.*

With monopodial growth, *the central stem grows in an upward direction on top of previous growth; aerial roots and flower stalks come from the central stem. Vanda and phalaenopsis have monopodial growth.*

Orchid flower structure:
1) petals, 2) sepals, 3) lip or
labellum, 4) throat, 5) column
(sometimes hidden by folds of
lip). Orchid pictured is popular
type of cattleya hybrid:
Brassolaeliocattleya Green
Lady 'Adagent'. Other cattleya
hybrids are discussed on
page 37.

water throughout the year; most epiphytes must be kept dry during some period of their growth cycle, usually either before or after flowering or at both times.

Two types of growth

Orchid plants, as they grow and enlarge from year to year, do so generally in one of two ways. Those with a *monopodial* type of growth become taller each year, the result of new growth only at the tip of the stem. Leaves are in two rows on opposite sides of the stem, the individual leaves alternating with those in the opposite row as they climb the stem. Flower spikes and aerial roots originate from the junction of leaf with stem or on the stem opposite a leaf.

The second basic growth type—and by far the most prevalent—is *sympodial.* Here, the upward growth of the plant stops, in most cases, after one growth season; the next year's growth comes from the base of usually the youngest growth. Sympodial orchids may bloom either from the tips of their most recent growth or from the sides or bases of it. Many sympodial orchids form pseudobulbs—thickened stems that serve as storage for food and water, making it possible for the plants to survive seasons of drought. Leaves may grow along the pseudobulbs or from their tips.

Foliage—not to be overlooked

Orchid foliage is usually tough, leathery, and succulent in texture as in the popular cattleyas, although occasionally it will be thin and papery as in various sobralias and coelogynes. Some species, like *Dendrobium nobile* and *D. pierardii,* lose their leaves after growth matures, but the vast majority are evergreen. Some orchids will be handsome foliage plants with masses of dark green leaves (cymbidiums are a familiar example); most species, however, are not particularly attractive when out of bloom.

Flowers—their structure and variety

Despite the complexity and variety of orchid flowers, their basic structure can be described simply. Three *sepals* and three *petals* constitute an orchid flower; the most spectacular aspect of many orchids—the intricately shaped and frequently colored lip—is no more than a highly modified petal. The *column,* containing the reproductive organs, is often hidden by part of the lip. Botanists use the column to distinguish orchids from other plant families.

Flowers are produced in several ways. Many species have pendent blossoms on long spikes; some may have a solitary flower at the end of an erect stem. Still other flowers are borne along upright stalks that may carry up to a hundred blooms altogether, or are carried in various numbers on upright, branching stems.

The variety of form in orchid flowers is remarkable. Some masdevallias look like small kites; catasetums give the illusion of birds in flight; *Anguloa cliftoni* resembles a tulip; *Coelogyne ocellata* looks like a miniature daisy. Such descriptive names as dove orchid (*Peristeria elata*), spider orchid (*Brassia caudata*), and moth orchid (*Phalaenopsis amabilis*) give some idea of the variety of imitative forms these flowers may take.

How to Grow Healthy Orchids

. . . simple guidelines for success

THERE are no longer any secrets about orchid growing, but there are some general rules to follow which, combined with common sense, can turn a brown thumb green. By their appearance and performance the orchid plants themselves will indicate their needs; it is up to you to recognize these signals from the plants and to understand their requirements.

The Temperature/Humidity Factor

Orchids may be conveniently grouped into general categories according to the temperatures they prefer for their best growth. The following three groups—cool, intermediate, and warm—are based on required winter night temperatures.

Cool-growing orchids prefer temperatures of 50° to 55°, rising to 60° to 70° during the day; this group includes cymbidiums, odontoglossums,

Profuse bloom *on Paphiopedilum Maori 'Oaklands' earned plant a Certificate of Cultural Merit from American Orchid Society. Other CCM winners include Cycnoches (facing page) and both orchids on page 10.*

and some paphiopedilums. Intermediate temperatures of 55° to 60° at night and 65° to 75° during the day are preferred for cattleyas, dendrobiums, some oncidiums, hybrid paphiopedilums, and many species orchids. And night temperatures of 60° to 65°, with 70° to 85° during the day, are ideal for warm-growing orchids such as vandas, phalaenopsis, and tropical paphiopedilums.

Fortunately, this does not mean that you must have separate rooms for those that prefer cool or warm temperatures. It is an easy matter to place some plants closer to the window where the temperature will be lower in winter; positions farther from the window pane will likely suit those that require more warmth.

Summer temperatures are frequently high, but a few days of excessive heat may not harm plants. If there is a long warm spell, try to keep plants as cool as possible. Outdoors, natural air currents constantly cool plants; in confined indoor areas excessive heat can be more harmful, especially if ventilation is poor.

You need not turn your home into a steaming jungle for your orchids. Most of these plants respond admirably when the amount of moisture in the air (humidity) is between 30 and 40 per cent—which is a healthy figure for people, too. A few species do need excessive humidity (as high as 80 per cent), but these are the exceptions rather than the rule. As temperatures lower in the evening, so should the humidity as a precaution against the disease organisms which thrive in cool temperatures and moisture (see page 14). To measure humidity, buy an inexpensive *hygrometer,* an instrument that measures moisture present in the air. Hygrometers are available from many hardware dealers.

Humidity is always easier to raise than it is to lower. Gravel-filled trays that catch excess water from routine waterings will provide some humidity as the water evaporates from the surface of the stones. Misting the air around plants with a spray gun also increases humidity as does the time-tested method of placing pans of water near radiators. During spring and summer you should mist orchids daily; decrease the frequency in autumn and winter.

A number of mist guns suitable for this purpose are available, but whether you use a window-cleanser bottle or an expensive sprayer you should never mist plants directly at close range. Instead, spray the area around the plants so that some moisture settles on the foliage but will evaporate by evening. You run the risk of diseased plants if water remains overnight on foliage or in crowns of plants (see page 14). If you have many plants growing together, the plants themselves will create additional humidity by their natural transpiration (see page 10).

Many furnace systems in newer homes are equipped with humidifiers. Where no such equipment exists, you can buy room humidifiers that will sufficiently increase humidity. These usually consist of a small motor-driven fan that breaks up water droplets into a fine mist.

Give Them Light and Air

In nature, orchids seldom grow in complete shade or where air is stagnant. Instead, they thrive in dappled sunlight and where there is a free circulation of air. A "fresh" atmosphere is essential if you want healthy flowering plants.

Air circulation in the home is generally satisfactory during summer because some windows are almost always open. In winter, however, if you cannot keep a window slightly ajar, use a small oscillating fan to keep air moving. Do not direct the fan at the plants, as they will not tolerate drafts; instead, position the fan so that the flow of air is directed above or below your orchids.

While there are many orchids that will thrive at a sunny window, the sun and light requirements do vary considerably among the various species and hybrids. Therefore, it is vital that you select plants which will perform best under the conditions you can provide. Do not, for example, place a sun-loving orchid in a shady location; it will not bloom. Conversely, a shade-loving plant grown in a sunny spot will likely develop leaf scorch. In both cases disappointment will result from unsatisfactory performance. Sometimes moving a plant only an inch or two—into more or less sun than it had been receiving—will make the difference between a healthy plant and one that simply exists.

Extraordinary flower spikes reflect the ideal care given to Cycnoches chlorochilon 'Green Glow'. Bright light and dry rest period are two important requirements.

How Much Water and Fertilizer?

There is no single rule which will tell you how often to water your orchids; their need for water depends upon several interacting factors. Knowledge of these, however, will allow you to determine the particular needs of your plants and to make adjustments as conditions change.

The sizes of containers in which your plants grow will determine the relative frequency of waterings needed, regardless of other conditions. Orchids in large pots (from 8 to 12 inches) dry out slowly; plants in smaller pots dry out more rapidly as the container size decreases. Baskets and slabs require water more often than containers with solid sides. The type of potting medium also helps determine plants' water requirements; fir bark dries more rapidly than osmunda fiber.

The amount of artificial heat indoors influences the orchids' demands for water: The more heat used, the more water plants will need. Even the weather outdoors exerts an influence. On cloudy days plants cannot use much water because transpiration rates are very low (transpiration is moisture a plant loses through its leaves). On hot sunny days, they will need abundant water to replenish moisture lost through the leaves.

Here's a convenient rule-of-thumb: when in doubt, don't water. Remember that most orchids have their own water reservoirs, and a few days without moisture will not be harmful. When watering your plants, always use tepid water—about 60°–70°.

Most orchids will tolerate a mild fertilizer (10-10-5) and various frequencies of application. Even so, two general guidelines will help you establish a fertilizing program for your plants. Orchids grown in fir bark will require more nitrogen than will plants in osmunda, and they will need to be fertilized more often. Plants need fertilizer least when they are not actively making new growth and when light intensity is low—during winter months and periods of cloudy weather.

Off to a Good Start

Throughout many years of experimentation, orchids have been grown in everything from coconut shreddings to charcoal and gravel. An ideal medium for all plants is difficult to find, as each medium has its inherent advantages and disadvantages. Fir bark is now the most popular orchid potting material in most regions; osmunda (the traditional medium) is still frequently used with great success but with less ease.

Fir bark is sold as chunks of bark which first have been graded according to size and then steamed to remove any toxic materials which may be present. If you use fir bark for potting your orchids, sift out dust, splinters, and other small particles that are sometimes mixed in during processing; if they remain they may impede drainage. The smallest grades are used for seedlings and miniature plants, medium grades for plants to 30 inches tall, and largest grades for larger plants like vandas and some brassias that prefer a very open growing medium.

Since fir bark contains virtually no nutrients, you may want to use a very weak solution of a commercial plant food every other watering during a plant's growing season. Fertilizers especially prepared for orchids are the simplest to use. In autumn and winter, fertilizing is usually unnecessary for most sorts; only those making new

Mammoth orchid has received proper culture for Angraecum: *diffused light, even moisture throughout year with rest period in autumn, and cattleya temperatures. This is* Angraecum sesquipedale 'Orchid Alley'.

Covered with blooms, Miltonia Bert Fields 'Riopelle' *shows benefit of good light, constant moisture, cool nights. Miltonias prefer 60 percent humidity. They flower best when crowded in pot.*

growth during these months will require it.

Bark is easy to work with and can be used wet or dry when potting plants, unlike osmunda which must be pre-moistened before use. Bark is also the best medium for getting roots growing quickly. Fir bark deteriorates within a year or two, and your plants will need to be repotted in fresh bark when this happens. Otherwise, much of the aeration and rapid drainage is sacrificed—to the detriment of the orchid roots.

Osmunda fiber is simply the aerial roots from two types of osmunda fern. The fiber holds water well, drying out slowly over a long period of time, and spaces between the fibers permit free circulation of air and drainage of excess water. Osmunda also contains more nutrients than does fir bark, so that plants in osmunda will require less additional feeding than will plants in bark. Usually within two to three years osmunda decays and must be replaced. So that it will be easy to handle when you pot your orchids in it, first soak osmunda overnight in water.

Terrestrial and semiterrestrial orchids like bletilla, pleione, and some paphiopedilums are best grown in a medium which consists of entirely organic materials. Chopped osmunda, leaf mold, and small grade fir bark (without removal of fine particles) in equal parts form a mixture that is generally satisfactory. A few orchids will even thrive in garden soil (see pages 28–29).

Choose your container

Orchids can be grown in any kind of container which has a hole for drainage in its base. Because ventilation around the bottom of the pot is vital to an orchid plant's well-being, excess water must not accumulate at the roots. For these reasons, slotted clay pots are made specifically for orchids; these are first-choice containers for your plants. If you use a standard clay pot (without the slotted base), enlarge the drainage hole by gently chipping away its edges.

A redwood basket with spaces between the laths is an ideal container for many species, especially plants of stanhopea and gongora which produce flower spikes that grow almost straight downward from the base of the plant. A wire basket, although perhaps not as pleasing esthetically, is another good choice for many orchids.

Plastic or glazed ceramic containers hold moisture over a much longer period of time than clay pots or baskets. Consequently you will have to guard against overwatering orchids grown in the non-porous containers. Fir bark, because it dries more rapidly than osmunda, is a better planting medium for orchids in plastic or glazed ceramic pots.

Some epiphytic orchids don't even need a container in which to grow. Miniatures and smaller species are often grown successfully on rafts or slabs of osmunda or tree fern fiber, or on pieces of bark or logs. These slabs may be suspended from ceiling hooks or hung on walls—duplicating an aerial environment from the wild.

Potting timetable

Following the blooming season and before new growth breaks there is usually a period of two to six weeks that is the optimum time for repotting. Then, the plants are at their most dormant stage and the necessary root disturbance will be felt the least.

A primer of potting

Orchids growing in 5, 6, 7, or 8-inch containers usually need repotting every eighteen months. By this time, those with a sympodial growth habit (see pages 6 and 7) will have begun to outgrow their containers and the bark or osmunda may have started to break down and lose its open texture. Larger plants (in larger containers) should not be disturbed for several years or until the potting material starts to lose its texture.

Specially made for orchids, this clay pot has enlarged slotted drainage holes.

Your first consideration in potting orchids is to be sure that containers are absolutely clean. Clay pots and the broken pieces of pots used for drainage material should be scrubbed in scalding water before use.

Removing a plant from its old container should be done with care; live roots may be damaged if you attempt to pull out or force the plant. Gently tap the outside of the pot with a hammer, or strike the pot's edge against a table top; this should free the root ball from the container. Gradually jiggle the plant out of its old potting mix, then shake off any remaining mix. Examine the root system of all plants and trim dead roots back to living tissue.

Potting in bark. Fill the bottom one-third of the container with pieces of broken pots, and set the plant in place. Then, fill in around the roots with fresh bark, occasionally pressing down the potting medium with a blunt-edged stick. Work from the sides of the pot to the center until you have filled the pot to within a half-inch of its rim. If necessary, stake the plant to hold it upright.

Potting in osmunda. The day before you plan to pot your orchids, soak the osmunda in water so it will be easy to handle. After it has soaked overnight, cut the osmunda into 3-inch squares with a sharp knife. Then, just as you would if you were potting in bark, fill the container about one-third full with pieces of broken pots and center the plant in place. Orchids grown in osmunda must have their roots tightly packed in the fiber. Start adding the osmunda at the edge of the pot and fill

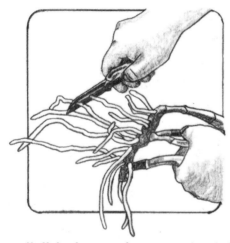

*1. **Cut off** all dead roots to live tissue after shaking off as much of old potting mix as possible.*

*2. **Place** cut end of division against edge of pot; divide plant if necessary (see page 17).*

*3. **Firm** the potting mix by pressing with fingers, blunt end stick, or by tapping pot.*

*4. **Stake plant** to hold upright; set in a warm location and out of direct sunlight.*

in around the roots. Work toward the center, packing the material in firmly. A blunt-ended potting stick will help you compact the osmunda. Continue to add osmunda until no more can be fitted in. Finally, trim away any excess fiber.

Potting in baskets or on slabs. When preparing baskets to receive orchid plants, line them with a thin layer of osmunda and then set plants in place as you would in an ordinary container. Adequate drainage is no problem in baskets, so you need not add the layer of broken pots before planting. If you plan to grow your orchids on slabs of tree fern, first wrap the roots in balls of osmunda. Tie the root ball to the slab with galvanized wire or string; when roots appear to have securely anchored plant to slab, you may cut away the wire or string.

For all newly-potted plants. After potting, set plants in a warm location (60° to 75°) and out of direct sunlight. Roots of most newly transplanted orchids are not capable of absorbing moisture immediately and may rot with too much water. For at least a week following planting, withhold water from the rooting medium; simply mist its surface and the outside of the pot. Following this

Variety of perches *for epiphytic orchids is almost unlimited. Shown here are cork oak bark (top) and compacted tree fern fiber (right).*

Slat-bottomed basket *provides good drainage, air circulation; is essential for orchids like stanhopea, whose flower spikes grow through the bottom.*

Sphagnum moss *provides foothold for roots of Oncidium pusillum; moss is wrapped around dead tree branch. Many miniatures can be mounted this way.*

 Growing healthy orchids **13**

PLANT PROBLEMS

SYMPTOM	PROBABLE CAUSE	REMEDY
Leaves turn yellow	Too much sunlight or water. Natural if only old leaves are involved	Move plant to a cool place; withhold water for a few weeks
Leaves turn yellow and fall	Natural with many deciduous types	Withhold water; move plant to a cool place to encourage bud formation
Leaves show black or brown areas	Too much sun; or infection by a leaf-spotting disease if spot grows	Move plant to more shade; or see text for disease control
Limp leaves, soft growth at base of plant	Waterlogged potting mixture	Withhold water; give plant a week with dry potting mix
No apparent sign of new growth	The time is not right, in the plant's growth cycle, for new growth	Keep potting mixture evenly moist; do not force plant with extra feeding or watering
Plant refuses to flower	Proper growth cycle and day-length not being observed	Determine times of year for plant's natural growth and rest periods; keep plant in darkness at night
Buds drop	Temperatures fluctuate too greatly	Move plant to a location having more even temperatures

initial "dry" period, begin watering sparingly. Resume normal watering only after you see that root or plant growth has started.

When Plants Need Help

Many plants, when poorly grown or carelessly handled, will fall easy victim to insects or disease. In this respect orchids are no different. However, with reasonable attention given to their basic needs their troubles will be few.

Your greatest asset in handling plant problems will be a sharp eye for any appearance or performance that seems abnormal. The check list on this page of possible problems will familiarize you with symptoms, causes, and remedies for troubles that arise from unfavorable growing conditions. In the following paragraphs are discussed the more common pests and disease organisms that are known to bother orchids.

Pests in your orchid collection can be identified by their damage. Chewed leaves may result from the activities of weevils, cattleya flies, sowbugs, springtails, snails, or slugs. Mottled or disfigured foliage usually indicates the presence of a sucking pest: scale, thrips, mealybugs, or spider mites.

Light infestations of many insects can be removed by hand or brushed away with a solution of soap and water. Only the microscopic insects (thrips and spider mites) or heavy populations of scale or mealybugs that have invaded hard-to-reach areas of the plants will require spraying with a pesticide.

Snails and slugs, if not removed by hand, are best controlled by a metaldehyde bait. Diazinon sprays will eradicate the other pests mentioned; a spray containing malathion is also satisfactory for these other pests.

Fungal and bacterial diseases are usually noticed as a collapse of the plant's tissues, frequently with a water-soaked appearance. Depending upon the disease, the part of the plant attacked may be leaves, stems, pseudobulbs, or roots.

Diverse as they are, these diseases are alike in requiring a high humidity to thrive. Some appear with humidity and low temperatures while others are not activated until temperatures are relatively high. To discourage disease organisms, water your orchids as early in the day as you can. By the time the temperature has reached its peak the plants will be dry, remaining so as the temperature falls for the night.

Should any plant become diseased despite

routine precautions, immediately isolate it from other healthy orchids. Cut out all diseased parts of the plant, sterilizing the tool after each cut to prevent its carrying the infection to other parts of the plant or to other healthy plants. To sterilize the tool, pass the blade through the flame of a Bunsen burner, alcohol lamp, or blow torch. Treat the cut surface with a fungicide: Natriphene (available from orchid specialists) or Bordeaux mixture (copper sulfate and lime) is satisfactory. Decrease water and humidity while the plant is recovering.

Virus infections in orchids may take innumerable forms, but they may generally be recognized by an abnormal patterning in the leaves. This patterning—often in yellow or shades of brown, and sometimes in watery streaks—may be reinforced by flowers which are streaked, malformed, or have colors broken into patches rather than smoothly blended, and which last but a fraction of their normal life. The symptoms may be obvious or they may be subtle. Have a suspicious plant checked at your nearest Agricultural Experiment Station.

Unfortunately, there is no cure for virus infections, and plants so affected *must* be destroyed. Insects and cutting tools can spread the virus to other healthy plants in a collection.

Viruses infect many different kinds of orchids, producing different symptoms in each. Here, cymbidium mosaic virus produces light pits on cattleya leaf. Same virus causes light and dark streaks on cymbidium.

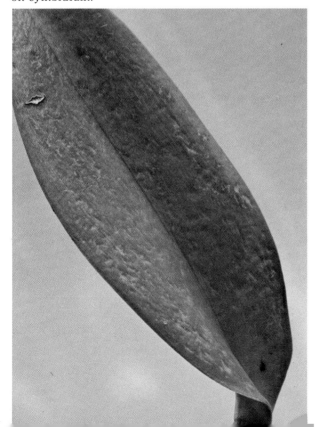

Sunburn causes soft, faded spots on leaves. These spots eventually turn brown, then black. Plants taken from shaded areas and placed in sunny windows are most quickly affected.

Soft scale insects create irregular crust on undersides of leaves and at junction of leaf and stem.

Brown rot begins as light brown spot on leaf and quickly spreads throughout plant.

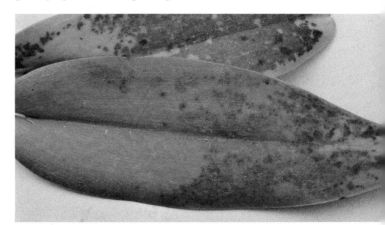

Bacterial leaf spot here produces sunken brown spots on cattleya leaves. Other kinds of leaf spots appear as yellow, brown, or reddish spots or streaks.

Increasing Your Collection

. . . how to shop wisely, propagate effectively

AFTER you have grown a few orchids, you will find that you want more. It is impossible to resist their beauty. But before you begin to buy additional plants you would be wise to plan your purchases. By so doing you will ultimately derive the greatest possible satisfaction for the money spent while keeping disappointments to a minimum.

Of the two "rules" which you should consider when purchasing new orchids, the first is to buy only plants that will thrive in the conditions you can offer them. If you have a warm growing area, concentrate on such kinds as vandas and phalaenopsis. If the area is cool, select miltonias, odontoglossums, and cymbidiums. Read the descriptions of these and other orchids on pages 30–63 to determine the plants' temperature tolerances.

The second "rule" to remember in any orchid purchase is to buy the best possible plants you can afford. This means that you should avoid both unhealthy bargain plants and those which bear inferior flowers for their type. Look for plants with healthy green growth and fresh white-tipped roots; these will be in prime shape to easily adjust to a new environment in your home. Healthy mature plants will give you the most enjoyment in the least amount of time.

For nurseries that specialize in orchid plants, see the list on page 20. Most growers are willing to give advice to make you a satisfied customer. They will be able to tell you if the orchid you want is fresh from the jungle and not yet established, and will, in such cases, probably suggest that you purchase something else.

New Plants From Old

Most orchids with a sympodial growth habit (see page 6) can be divided, as you might divide bulbs, to produce more plants of the same kind. Divide the plant by severing with a sharp sterile knife the rhizome at the point where the cut will leave 4 pseudobulbs or stems to each division. Then carefully pull apart the mass of roots. Such a strong division will establish itself so rapidly that blossoms may be borne on the next year's growth.

Don't throw away orchid stems or old "back bulbs" (those pseudobulbs, taken from the rear of the plant, that no longer bear leaves); many times they can be induced to grow new shoots by placing them partially buried in damp sand or vermiculite in a warm place. Be sure to leave the growing eye or bud (at the base of the pseudobulb, or at the nodes on stems) exposed to the air. Plants produced from back bulbs or stems generally require 3 to 5 years to mature.

Rooted "keikis" (Hawaiian for babies) *can be cut from this dendrobium and potted.*

(Continued on page 19)

Explosion of color surrounds customer at orchid nursery—shown here are cattleyas, epidendrum, phalaenopsis, miltonias, and oncidium. These orchids are available from commercial growers, who can also be valuable sources of information for both beginner and more advanced grower. You'll find list of orchid nurseries on page 20.

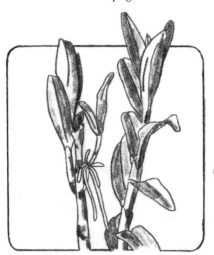

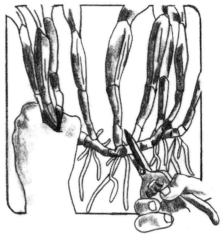

Offshoots (keikis) are produced on stems, flower spikes, or from bases of many orchids. Cut off and pot when young roots are well developed.

Back bulbs from cymbidiums may produce new plants from dormant buds when potted in bark, sand, or vermiculite. Keep bud above surface of potting mix.

Divisions can be separated with sterilized clippers or knife. Make cuts in the old rhizome so that each new division will have four pseudobulbs.

The Art of Making a Corsage

You don't need the skill of a florist to produce a professional-appearing corsage using your own orchids. As few as a dozen plants, selected for consecutive seasons of bloom, can furnish corsage orchids almost the year around.

Because of their long-lasting qualities, orchids make superior corsage flowers. Almost any orchid can be used for this purpose. The flowers are so lovely that cutting them from the plant will take courage at first, but as your collection grows the temptation to use your own flowers will win out.

So that the flowers will have their full color, cut them after they have been open on the plant for a few days. Use a sterile razor and cut flower stems off at the base. Then cut a thin, angled slice from the end of each stem. This allows the stem to take up water more readily than does a cut made directly across the stem.

With 1 to 1½ inches of stem remaining on the flower, insert florist wire through the stem, near the flower. Bend the wire down along each side of the stem and twist a second wire around both stem and wire in a spiral. Using green floral tape, securely wrap the stem and the first few inches of the wire that extends beyond it. For a multi-flower corsage, wrap several wired flowers together with floral tape.

In corsages of single flowers the orchid should be worn right side up—as it naturally grows. When corsages contain several flowers, at least one—preferably the dominant flower—should be in its natural position.

Ribbon bows can be effective complements to orchid blooms, but use ribbon sparingly to avoid detracting from the flowers. In pinning a corsage to clothing, secure the pin through the ribbon—not through the stem.

While it is being worn, the stem of the flower can be inserted in a glass vial of water to keep it fresh. Vials for this purpose (available from florist suppliers) have a rubber cap with a hole through which you insert the stem for its entire length. If you cannot locate glass vials, you can encase the stem in moist cotton, then wrap it in plastic. For better appearance, the plastic-wrapped cotton can be covered with floral tape.

When the corsage is not being worn, put the flowers in a refrigerator where the temperature will not be lower than 45°. A refrigerator's vegetable compartment will usually provide the proper conditions. Stems can be left in the glass vial or moistened cotton. Placed on a bed of shredded wax paper in a plastic bag, orchid flowers will remain fresh for many days if the opening of the bag is securely folded shut.

Next stop, a lovely shoulder. You need not be a florist to make this corsage. It's an easy job to twist florist wire for decorative effect and add pins (small white beads) and complementary ribbon.

Old stems of dendrobiums can be cut into small sections and placed on moist sphagnum moss to encourage plantlets to develop. Plantlets produced naturally on the plant can be separated from the stem and potted as soon as roots form.

Monopodial orchids (those that grow vertically rather than horizontally) can also be propagated by the amateur orchid grower. Side shoots develop on many monopodial orchids. They can be removed after they have started their own roots. Sometimes plantlets, called *keikis*, form on flower spikes. Pot these plantlets and then enclose pot and all in a plastic bag. Clumps of paphiopedilums are easily divided into more specimens. Rather than cut the rhizome, use your fingers to break it with a twist. Leave three growths to a division.

Meristem culture is a specialized method of rapidly increasing individual plants, especially those of a scarce new hybrid. From the plant's growing tip, the embryonic growth cell is removed and cultured in a nutrient solution where it reproduces itself many times. Later, these cells are separated into individual flasks in which they grow into seedling-sized plants identical to that from which the original growth cell was taken. Hybrids reproduced in this manner may be designated "mericlones."

Seedlings: from flask to flowering

Growing orchids from seed is a time consuming process best left to experienced specialists. However, you can buy flasks of small seedling plants ready to be transferred to community pots. You will ultimately have the pleasure of seeing your own unique seedlings produce their first flowers, but without having to be involved with the laboratory procedures needed for germinating the seeds.

Many orchid suppliers offer flasks of seedlings which contain about 200 tiny plants. These plantlets are ready to come out of the flask when they are about ½ inch high; usually they are this size when you buy them.

Some commercial orchid growers offer a "custom seeding service" which is an advantage to amateur orchid enthusiasts who want to raise seedlings from particular parent plants but who lack the facilities to germinate the seeds. For an established fee, the grower will germinate the seeds from the seed capsule which you take to him; you get the seedling plants when they are large enough to be removed from the seedling flasks to a community pot.

The community pot

Before removing seedlings from their flask for potting, you should assemble all the materials you will need for the operation. A number of 3 to 5-inch pots (well-scrubbed and dipped in boiling water, if they have been used before) should be soaked in water for several hours so that they will not extract any water from the potting mix. When this is completed and the pots are ready for use, fill the pots about ⅓ full with clean pieces of broken pottery and then add a potting mixture of a seedling grade fir bark combined with the material screened out of a coarser grade. Pack the mix tightly into the pot and water it.

To remove the seedlings from the flask, pour ½

Orchid seedlings begin their lives in flasks of sterilized agar with nutrients for growth. When big enough, seedlings go to community pots.

cup of room-temperature water into the flask. Swirl the flask; then pour out the loosened seedlings into a shallow bowl. Repeat this process until all seedlings are out.

Planting the seedlings is the easiest part of the operation. Punch small holes in the potting mixture with the tip of a pencil and set the tiny plants in place. About 20 to 30 plants can be accommodated in a community pot.

Spring is the best time of year for moving seedlings. This gives them the greatest possible amount of time to grow before any dormant period in fall or winter.

Seedlings in their first community pot require a humid location and a relatively constant temperature in the 67°–80° range. A greenhouse satisfies their needs easily. Lacking this, the home orchid grower can buy or easily make a small glass case to house the pots of seedlings. Even a packing box with a glass pane over the top may be suitable. Whatever you use, the seedlings should be placed in a bright but not sunny spot.

Never allow the potting mixture to dry out, but remember that a soggy condition is just as unsatisfactory. Once-a-day watering will probably be necessary, but this should be done early enough so that foliage will be dry before twilight to avoid encouraging diseases. On sunny days the seedlings will benefit from a fine misting during the day, but early enough so that leaves can dry before dusk. Open the seedlings' enclosure for an hour or two each day to allow air to circulate in and around the plants.

Time to transplant

It will be about a year (depending upon the orchid species grown) before the seedlings are ready for transplanting. For this second move, put 3 to 6 plants into a clean 3-inch pot in the same type potting mix. Give them more light and some weak fertilizer once a month.

In another year or so, when the plants start to crowd one another, they are ready for individual pots. Transplant them into small grade fir bark or into osmunda in 2 or 3-inch containers.

A final transplanting is necessary, after about one more year, at which time they should go into individual 5-inch pots in medium grade fir bark. Most plants will flower in these pots.

If the above procedure seems lengthy to you, buy orchids in the 2 or 3-inch pot stage. Plants will be sturdy and will have passed the most cru-

cial time of their lives; they will be about 3 years old (from seed), ready for their third transplanting. Depending on the vigor of the plants, a fourth potting will bring them up to blooming size.

Shopping for Orchids

Many general nurseries carry a few orchids for sale, but the largest and most varied selections of orchid species and hybrids will be found at nurseries that specialize in these plants. The following list includes a few of the largest growers that publish catalogs or price lists and can ship plants to you. For some catalogs there will be a small charge.

Alberts & Merkel Bros., Inc. 2210 South Federal Highway, Boynton Beach, FL 33435.

Armacost & Royston, Inc., 3376 Foothill Road, P.O. Box 385, Carpenteria, CA 93013.

The Beall Company, P.O. Box 467, Vashon Island, WA 98070

Black River Orchids, P.O. Box 110, South Haven, MI 49090.

Breckinridge Orchids, 6201 Summit Avenue, Brown Summit, NC 27214

John Ewing Orchids, P.O. Box 384, Aptos, CA 95003.

Great Lakes Orchids, Inc., 28805 Pennsylvania Road, Romulus, MI 48174.

Orchids by Hausermann, Inc., 2N 134 Addison Road, Villa Park, IL 60181.

Hirose Nurseries, Hilo, HI 96720.

Jones & Scully, Inc., 18955 S.W. 168th Street, Miami, FL 33187.

Rainforest Orchids, 1408 Route 539, Warren Grove, NJ 08005.

Rod McLellan Orchids, 1450 E. Camino Real, South San Francisco, CA 94080.

Shaffer's Tropical Gardens, 1220 41st Street, Capitola, CA 95010.

Fred A. Stewart, Inc., P.O. Box 307, San Gabriel, CA 91778.

Zuma Canyon Orchids, 5949 Bonsall Drive, Malibu, CA 90265.

Understanding Orchid Names

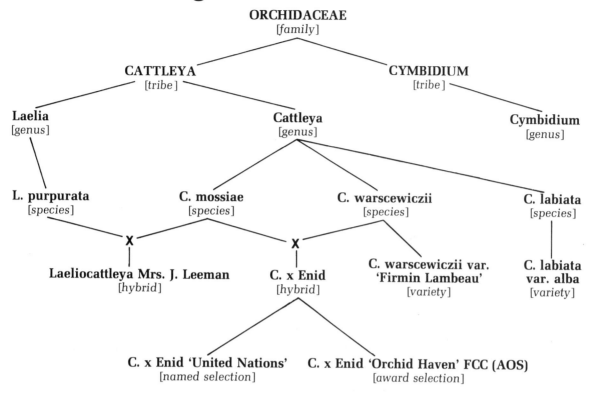

ORCHIDACEAE
[family]

CATTLEYA
[tribe]

CYMBIDIUM
[tribe]

Laelia
[genus]

Cattleya
[genus]

Cymbidium
[genus]

L. purpurata
[species]

C. mossiae
[species]

C. warscewiczii
[species]

C. labiata
[species]

X

X

Laeliocattleya Mrs. J. Leeman
[hybrid]

C. x Enid
[hybrid]

C. warscewiczii var.
'Firmin Lambeau'
[variety]

C. labiata
var. alba
[variety]

C. x Enid 'United Nations'
[named selection]

C. x Enid 'Orchid Haven' FCC (AOS)
[award selection]

The orchid *family* has been organized by botanists into a number of *genera,* each of which (called a *genus*) contains from one to many *species* which show a close relationship to one another. These genera are placed into larger groups called *tribes.* Thus, the orchids *Laelia anceps* and *Laelia purpurata* are distinct species but with enough characteristics in common to be included in the same genus, *Laelia.* The genera *Laelia* and *Cattleya* have similarities that place them in the same tribe.

When two orchid species are crossed, the hybridizer gives that cross a name which all seedlings from that cross are entitled to bear, regardless of who else might make the same cross or how many years later he or she might make it. For example, all hybrids of *Cattleya mossiae* x *Cattleya warscewiczii* are identified as Cattleya x Enid; the "x" preceding Enid indicates that the plant so named is a hybrid.

Because plants from the same parents will all differ from one another to some extent, the hybrid name is not a guarantee of quality but only of ancestry. Really fine hybrid plants can be further designated in two ways: The hybrid name will be followed by a selection name that is enclosed in single quotation marks (for example, Cattleya x Enid 'United Nations') or, if a hybrid has received an award, the

award initials following the selection name will designate this superior plant. The special feature on page 25 elaborates on these awards.

Within the orchid family, members of different genera can often cross with greater ease than is possible in other plant families. As a result, a number of intergeneric hybrids have been produced. To designate these hybrids, the genus name is replaced by a name coined from the names of the genera which produced the hybrid. Laeliocattleya x Mrs. J. Leeman, therefore, is a hybrid between a laelia species and a species of cattleya. For use in cases where so many genera are involved in a hybrid's background that the coined name becomes unmanageable, a set of "code names" has been internationally established to indicate hybrids of particular intergeneric backgrounds. *Potinara* is the coined "genus name" for hybrids involving rhyncholaelia, cattleya, laelia, and sophronitis, though jawbreakers like *Dialaeliocattleya* still exist.

Any species will exhibit some variation from plant to plant in the wild, so it is natural that orchid growers should want to propagate an especially good representative of unexpected color variation of a species. The abbreviation "var." (for "variety") indicates a selected form.

Growing Orchids Indoors

. . . equally easy at a window or under lights

WHETHER you live in a city apartment or a home in the country, whether you have a greenhouse, a sunny window, or grow plants in a basement under artificial lights, there are many orchids you can grow successfully. If you have limited space for plants, choose from the delightful miniature or dwarf species and hybrids that grow no more than 12 inches tall; if a window sill is your growing area, make your selections from the thousands of medium-size plants that may reach 30 inches. For a special place or for patio decoration, larger plants are available. With some 25,000 species and an equal number of hybrids, there are plants for every place in almost any situation.

Orchids at the Window

Plants that will not exceed 30 inches in height are the most satisfactory choices for the average window. Six or seven of them, carefully selected, will present a colorful scene almost all year. For your greatest pleasure, avoid those species that have less than attractive growth habits, and always select plants that will adapt themselves to the growing environment you can provide.

Select a bright window, preferably east or south. Make sure that most of the sunlight coming through is not direct; it should be filtered or reflected light so as not to burn the foliage. Unlike many other house plants, orchids rarely attract insects, so it is seldom necessary to use insecticides indoors.

. . . or under Artificial Light

Today legions of indoor gardeners grow plants under lights. Otherwise useless spaces in attics, basements, and poorly-lighted rooms have been transformed into lush greeneries by enterprising gardeners who lack the proper window space to grow quantities of plants. If you choose not to make your own artificial light setup, you may choose from various manufactured fixtures.

Combine the right kind of artificial light (for the correct length of time and at the right intensity) with proper cultural methods, and you can make orchids flourish in any home or apartment. Special fluorescent lamps for growing plants are sold at many hardware stores and garden supply centers.

Research has shown that blue and red portions of the light spectrum are the wave lengths most needed by plants for photosynthesis—the manufacture of food by the plants; fluorescent lights provide these wave lengths. In addition, the far-red rays trigger many growth and flowering responses; these are emitted by ordinary incandescent bulbs. Therefore, a combination of fluorescent and incandescent lights is generally used by most gardeners, at a 5 to 1 ratio: 5 watts of fluorescent to 1 watt of incandescent.

Because orchids are basically high light-intensity plants, a minimum of four 40-watt fluorescent tubes and four 8-watt incandescent bulbs is recommended for successful growing. Extended service bulbs are better than standard ones because they produce more far-red rays and last longer than standard bulbs. You can buy fluorescent fixtures that have reflectors and sockets for incandescent bulbs.

Cool white or daylight fluorescent lamps can be used, but for higher light intensities lamps specifically designed for growing plants are available. Once you have decided on your arrangement and the necessary tubes, you may want to call an electrician to assemble the unit.

Using the four-lamp, 40-watt arrangement with incandescent light included, keep light-loving orchids such as epidendrums, cattleyas, and oncidiums as close to the lamps as possible; a distance of 3 inches is entirely satisfactory. Plants that need less light—phalaenopsis, paphiopedilums, and coelogynes—should be placed 12 inches below the tubes. With any arrangement, adjusting plants to the light source is easy; with the light source 12 inches above all plants, those needing more light may be placed on platforms or inverted pots to bring them to the required distance.

Generally, 14 hours of artificial light each day throughout the year is an acceptable length to maintain in the beginning. However, some plants will need a longer exposure to light and others will require less to achieve the optimum environment. To determine the most favorable light duration for your various orchids will require some experimentation and careful observation of the results. It takes orchids many months to become accustomed to artificial light, so do not be disheartened if you lose a few plants at the start. Once adjusted, they will grow easily.

Under artificial lights—just as when grown in natural light—orchids require good ventilation, humidity, and proper watering. Although each gardener will eventually work out a cultural program suited to his particular situation, you will find it best to begin by keeping plants at a daytime temperature of 78° to 85° with a drop of 15 degrees at night. Try to provide 40 to 50 per cent humidity in the growing area and *be sure plants receive*

Spray of phalaenopsis, grown in greenhouse, *adds lively touch to room decor. Collection of only a dozen plants can give you color all year.*

Light through generous window *enhances growing environment. Here, southeastern exposure has proved just right. Slightly ajar, windows allow good air circulation and prevent overheating.*

Simple yet elegant, this setting features miniature cymbidium brought indoors at its flowering peak.

blooms shaped to form an oval or an ellipse, yet giving the appearance of one flower. For admirers of the minute, there are also species whose flowers must be seen through a magnifying glass for the greatest appreciation of their intricate beauty.

Many miniature orchids adjust slowly to new conditions, and it is not unlikely that you might experience a few losses. It will take about six months before they become really established. Until you see that they are beginning to grow and establish themselves, it is best to water them sparingly (about once a week) and keep them at a bright window where temperatures range from around 70° to 75°.

Because most miniatures come in 1 or 2-inch thumbnail pots of osmunda which dry out rapidly, you must water them daily. For easier growing, put a group that requires the same environment in a large pot to minimize the danger of rapid drying. A number of plants could also be accommodated on a tree fern slab. Wire a patch of osmunda to the slab, and on this cushion fasten the plants. Then prop the slab against a window frame so that it will rest in a deep clay saucer that will catch excess water. Tree fern slabs may also be suspended from the ceiling if you have beneath them a catch basin for excess water, or if you take them down and water the slabs at the sink.

Whenever you grow miniatures together—in a large pot or on tree fern slabs—select species that require similar growing conditions.

Any of these miniature orchids are available from specialty nurseries; see the listing on page 20. For more information on how to grow them, read the individual plant descriptions on pages 32 to 62.

Popular miniatures include *Cattleya walkeriana, Dendrobium aggregatum, D. a. jenkinsii, Oncidium pusillum,* and species of *Ascocentrum, Bulbophyllum, Maxillaria, Pleurothallis, Rodriguezia,* and *Trichocentrum.*

Orchids that grow to 30 inches. If you have space to accommodate larger plants, here are some to consider: *Brassavola, Brassia, Cattleya, Coelogyne, Cycnoches,* miniature *Cymbidium, Dendrobium, Epidendrum* (particularly *Encyclia*), *Laelia, Lycaste, Miltonia, Mormodes, Odontoglossum, Oncidium, Paphiopedilum, Phalaenopsis, Stanhopea,* and *Zygopetalum.*

Orchids that grow over 4 feet. *Aerides* and *Vanda* hybrids are for people who have lots of window space. Be sure and check the individual plant descriptions, pages 43–44, for the kind of growing conditions they prefer.

adequate ventilation. Overcrowding and a stuffy atmosphere in an artificial light garden will invite disease and disappointment.

Orchids to Grow Indoors

Many orchids can be successfully grown indoors. The following list includes those that adapt best to an indoor environment. Since many orchids are raised in a greenhouse, your new plants may receive a jolt when brought indoors. They may wilt, loose a few leaves, or drop flower buds. Don't panic; mist them regularly, water as you would normally, but don't add fertilizer—it can add to the jolt. Once the orchids become acclimated and new growth appears, you can begin regular fertilizing.

Miniature orchids. Limited growing space need not deny you the pleasure of growing a number of orchids in your home. The many miniature species and hybrids need little space to produce their typically beautiful and exotic blossoms. Because the plants are small, do not think the flowers are insignificant. Some are large and breathtaking; other species may have a series of smaller

Awards of the American Orchid Society

While shopping in an orchid nursery or looking through a catalog, you'll often find an abbreviation—FCC/AOS, for example—at the end of a variety's name. What does the abbreviation mean? It means the American Orchid Society (AOS) has judged that variety to be an outstanding orchid and has presented it with an award.

The AOS regularly grants these awards to exceptional plants or flowers. The society's certified judges conduct award sessions at regional conferences, regional monthly judging sessions, and annual shows. Most of the orchids pictured in this book are AOS award winners.

By understanding the qualities AOS judges consider while judging an award-winning orchid, you may better appreciate the orchids you see, the orchids you want, and the orchids you already have. The knowledge will also be useful if you decide to enter your own orchids for judging.

When considering individual flowers of new varieties, the judges evaluate form (or shape), color, size, and substance (thickness or waxiness). A round, full flower is one quality of an award winner (flatness, as well as roundness, of the flower is the goal for miltonias, phalaenopsis, and vandas).

Colors must be definite and clear. In multihued orchids, colors should be in well-defined areas and patterns, with any blending of colors being regular and harmonious—not muddy.

The size of the orchid should be an improvement over the average size of the orchid's parents. Substance of the flower, too, must exceed that of the parents, with very heavy substance being the accepted ideal for some types.

If it's deemed perfect in every respect, an orchid will receive a score of 100 on the judges' point scale; for any imperfections, points are deducted. When an orchid receives 90 or more points from this possible 100, the AOS awards the First Class Certificate (FCC for short)—the top honor given by the AOS to an orchid. The miltonia pictured above was such a winner, as was the odontoglossum on page 2.

With a score of at least 80 points but below 90, an orchid earns the Award of Merit (designated AM). A few AM/AOS winners we show are the phalaenopsis on page 2, the oncidium on page 31, *Cymbidium* Starbright on page 39, the *Vandanthe* on page 42, and the *Colmanara* on page 50.

Orchids with scores below 80 but above 75 earn a

Clear, definite color helps make Miltonia *Anjou* 'Red Mask' winner of FCC, top AOS award.

Highly Commended Certificate (HCC)—it is this commendation that most award-winning orchids receive. Some examples are the cattleya on page 31, the odontioda on page 50, and *Paphiopedilum* Tommie Hanes on page 55.

Another major award of the society is the Certificate of Cultural Merit (CCM), which is given to well-grown plants—those that are of good size, are in prime condition, and have an unusually large number of quality flowers. Because these orchids need not be outstanding new hybrids or varieties, the chances are good for even a beginning orchid grower to come away with this award. Pages 8, 9, and 10 show four examples of CCM winners.

While the immediate value of judging is to recognize these exceptional orchids, the American Orchid Society grants awards also to encourage worthwhile trends in hybridizing. The result: better and more beautiful orchids for all of us.

Orchids under Glass

. . . greenhouse care for finicky favorites

WHILE you do not need a greenhouse to grow orchids, a special place for them with controlled conditions is a convenience. The plants growing together increase the humidity, and watering is easy as there is no concern for where excess water will go. The greenhouse may be a simple lean-to structure, a more elaborate separate building, a garden room incorporated into the house, or even a glassed-in enclosure projecting from a window. Many fine greenhouses have been constructed from salvaged materials.

Shop around before selecting a greenhouse. You can send for catalogs from greenhouse manufacturers to see what's available, visit local greenhouse manufacturers, or ask friends or neighbors who already have greenhouses. You may also wish to consult the *Sunset* book *Greenhouse Gardening*.

Five factors need to be considered when you grow orchids in a greenhouse: light, heating, humidity, cooling and ventilation, and watering. These interior climate controls will determine which orchids you can grow best.

Light. While plentiful light is one of the basic requirements in successful orchid culture, too much light is to be avoided; leaf scorch and desiccation of plants will be the result. Since most greenhouses are all glass, you must control the light with shades or shading compounds (whitewash) on the glass, especially in summer and sometimes in winter in all-year temperate climates. Few orchids will tolerate sun all year.

Heating. In areas where winter temperatures regularly drop below 45°, you'll find a heating system essential. Several heating devices manufactured for greenhouse use are available, and the one you

Phalaenopsis and related orchids *show off well in home greenhouse. Translucent glass roof allows just right amount of light to reach orchids. Heater and humidifier fit below benches in rear.*

choose depends upon your individual climate. Most greenhouse manufacturers also supply heating systems; study the literature carefully to decide which unit is best for your needs.

Humidity. Excessive humidity must also be guarded against in the greenhouse. Too much moisture in the air coupled with gray days is an invitation for diseases to invade. Keep humidity in the growing area between 40 and 60 per cent.

There are several types of automatic humidifiers available. Many of these operate in conjunction with cooling or air circulation systems.

Cooling and ventilation. Be certain that there is *always* good ventilation to provide the all-important air circulation. Strive for a "fresh" atmosphere in the greenhouse. In some instances you may need to cool the air as well as keep it moving.

The simplest ventilation system is a series of vents along the roof and at the base of the greenhouse. These vents can be operated manually or, if you wish to invest the time and money, be opened and closed automatically.

Bottom ventilation will also contribute greatly to the health of your orchids. Greenhouse benches which are constructed from slats with spaces between each will provide for this important air circulation.

During hot summer weather when ventilation and cooling are especially important, you may

Double-chambered greenhouse separates orchids that require different temperature ranges.

need to utilize an evaporative cooler and fan system. More elaborate systems are available, but necessary only if you live in a very hot climate or if you plan to grow cool-temperature orchids (see page 8).

Watering. The frequency of watering greenhouse orchids depends upon many interacting factors, and also upon the needs of the particular orchids you grow. Basically, most orchids should be liberally watered in spring and summer and not so much during the rest of the year. Fogging and misting is always beneficial; this can be done several times a day in hot weather to keep plants cool but is needed less during fall and winter.

If you water your greenhouse orchids with a garden hose, you may have to use a spray nozzle or bubbler attachment; a strong jet of water from the hose can wash away potting mix and expose plant roots.

Simplest greenhouse is a lean-to attached to another structure. Place greenhouse to receive all-day sun.

Orchid Beauty Outdoors

. . . selected varieties can thrive in your garden

GARDENERS in temperate parts of California and Florida and in all of Hawaii can use orchids in their landscapes. Some orchids will grow directly in the ground; others are better suited to containers where they can function as portable accent pieces. While cymbidiums, cattleyas, dendrobiums, and vandas are most often seen outdoors, there are a number of other orchids described in this chapter that can provide color for your garden. In raised beds, you can have orchids as a spring or summer display in the same way you would use perennials or annuals. If you grow these orchids in containers you can continually shift new plants to display beds as they come into bloom.

In regions where summers are short, leave your orchids in their containers so they can be moved to shelter when the weather becomes unfavorable. In these cold areas, set plants outdoors from May through October. Hang pots or baskets from branches or place them strategically on the patio or terrace, but don't make the mistake of placing plants directly on trees; it takes almost a year for an orchid to become established on a branch, making this practice impossible in all but the mild winter climates.

If you do shift your tender orchids outdoors during the warm summer months, be sure to adjust them gradually to the outdoor atmosphere. See directions for this under "Orchids for the Patio," facing page.

Orchids in the Ground

Terrestrial orchids demand a well-drained soil. Prepare beds by digging down at least 18 inches and replace the existing soil with a mix of equal parts garden loam and pulverized osmunda. A location that faces south or east is best, though some species will bloom in a west-facing area. Cool and shaded north exposures should be avoided for all but the few (such as pleione and cypripedium) that require constant moisture combined with a cool atmosphere.

Orchids for Near-Tropical Regions

Gardeners in these continually warm and frequently moist areas have the greatest range of orchids from which to choose to decorate their gardens. Almost literally, the world is their greenhouse.

In southern Florida and in the Hawaiian Islands, local growers will offer a number of species and hybrids that you can grow outside in your garden.

Hardy terrestrial *species* Bletilla striata *is readily available and easy to grow.*

Cymbidiums in flower are outstanding patio subjects in winter and spring. Here, containers are concealed by potted azaleas and cyclamen.

Orchids for Temperate Gardens

Which orchids are good risks for these gardens depends upon the definition of "temperate." Some of the orchids in the following list will survive temperatures down to freezing but not below it; others will take varying degrees of frost. Temperature tolerances are indicated for each genus described: *Bletilla*, to 20°; *Cymbidium*, to 28°; *Epidendrum*, to 28°; *Habenaria*, low 20's; *Laelia*, to mid-30's; *Pleione*, to 10°.

Orchids for Cold Winter Regions

If winter temperatures are likely to drop to 20° or lower for any extended periods, you can assume you have a cold winter climate for orchids. Some species described in the preceding section of "Orchids for Temperate Gardens" will endure your cold weather, but your choice is more limited. With the exception of species of *Pleione*, your selection includes only native North American species. These natives are obtainable from a number of sources. It's wise to buy propagated plants rather than those that are collected from the wild. For more information, read the conservation notes on page 45.

Orchids for the Patio

Most orchids are tropical in appearance and will lend an exotic air to your terrace or patio. Species and hybrids that bloom during spring and summer will, of course, be enjoyed the most during the outdoor-living months.

Before setting plants outdoors, prepare them for brighter light than they are accustomed to receiving inside. To do this, first put them in a somewhat shady place, then move them to dappled sunlight for a few days, and finally shift them into direct sun. Observe leaves to be sure they are not being scorched from too much sun. Plants will appreciate frequent sprayings with water, as long as this moisture is gone by dusk.

The following orchids, suitable for growing outdoors during the months when temperatures remain above 50°, will provide you with colorful flowers at that time (see pages 30–56 for descriptions): *Aerides* species, *Brassia* species, *Cattleya* hybrids, *Dendrobium* species and hybrids, *Epidendrum* species and hybrids, *Miltonia* hybrids, *Odontoglossum grande*, *Oncidium sarcodes*, *Vanda teres*, and *V. tricolor suavis*.

Outdoors, orchid plants benefit greatly from natural air currents and rain, but you should attempt to keep plants evenly moist. During sunny weather you may have to water them daily because the free-flowing air outdoors will evaporate moisture quickly. The best type of location for orchids is a sheltered area where there is some sunlight. Since orchids like bottom ventilation, potted plants used outdoors should not be placed directly on the ground or patio floor. You can easily make platforms of redwood laths for your container-grown orchids or place the pots on bricks spaced an inch or more apart.

A Galaxy of Star Performers

. . . plus some lesser-known starlets

THE orchid family offers a vast range of flower and plant forms, each with specific growing needs. To start a collection, look for orchids that do well in the growing conditions you can provide.

The beginner will probably recognize the four favorites: cattleya, cymbidium, paphiopedilum, and phalaenopsis. Many other, less familiar orchids also make good choices at first. Experienced growers can try new or more exotic orchids.

The orchids listed in this section are among the most widely grown. Many of them should be available from orchid nurseries or mail-order catalogs (see page 20 for a listing); some—especially the named varieties—may require a more diligent search. Because of continuing hybridization, named orchid varieties come and go rapidly. The varieties pictured in this book are representative of the wide selection of flower colors and forms available.

How orchids are classified

Botanists divide this large family of plants into more manageable groups called tribes; a tribe consists of related genera of orchids (for more information see "Understanding Orchid Names," page 21). The orchids within each tribe share physical characteristics and have similar growing needs.

The orchid groups presented here are popular with beginning growers. Still, within each group you can find more unusual orchids too.

Orchids that are not members of the most common tribes are grouped together under "Botanicals" (pages 58–63). These orchids represent tribes that may have as few as one commonly known member.

Intergeneric hybrids

The diversity of flower forms, colors, and sizes already present in the orchid family has not stopped growers from creating new forms, colors, and sizes to add to the collection. Hybridizers have gone beyond the comparatively subtle changes that occur in variety and species hybrids (see page 21). They now combine desirable traits from such contrasting genera as the large, clambering *Vanda* and the compact dwarf *Ascocentrum*. The resulting intergeneric hybrid, called an *Ascocenda*, is a small plant that yields relatively large vandalike flowers.

Concluding the plant listings for the Cattleya, Aerides, and Odontoglossum tribes are examples of intergeneric hybrids. They are only a selection from the more than 200 hybrid genera known.

New names for old orchids

You may see new, unfamiliar names for some well-known orchids in this listing. These name changes reflect studies of contemporary orchidologists whose task it is to clarify orchid relationships. In cases in which a new name is preferable, the older, more familiar name is placed in parentheses after the new name. For example, the orchid *Brassavola digbyana* is now labeled *Rhyncholaelia digbyana* (*Brassavola digbyana*).

A starting selection

Until you feel sure of yourself, it's a good idea to start with some not-so-fussy plants. This list of easy-to-grow orchids will provide you with some guidelines when you shop for the first time. Usually, all of these are readily available and inexpensive: *Bletilla striata, Brassavola nodosa, Cattleya labiata* and its myriad of varieties and hybrids, *Cymbidium* hybrids, *Dendrobium bigibbum phalaenopsis, Epidendrum ibaguense, Laelia anceps, Paphiopedilum insigne,* P. *Maudiae, Phalaenopsis* white-flowered hybrids, and *Pleione.* Be sure to check the growing needs of these orchids to make sure you can provide the necessary conditions.

Cattleya Lovely 'Beauty'

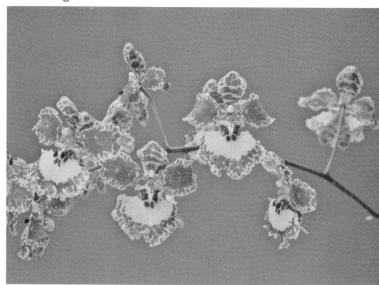

Oncidium gardnerii 'Lil'

Phalaenopsis Zwingli 'Pink Champion'

The Major Orchid Groups

After familiarizing yourself with different orchid groups, you'll find it easier to give proper care to your orchids. The cattleya, cymbidium, and dendrobium pictured represent their namesake groups. The phalaenopsis belongs in the Aerides group, the oncidium in the Odontoglossum group, and the paphiopedilum in the Cypripedium group.

Cymbidium Bali 'Champagne'

Paphiopedilum Alderbrook 'San Juan'

Dendrobium Gatton Monarch 'Rickey's'

31

Cattleya tribe

This easily grown, popular group of orchids contains a large number of species and hybrids. It includes the familiar *Cattleya* (the genus), the varied *Epidendrum,* and the delicately beautiful yet little-known *Caularthron.*

Cattleyas are native to the Americas, particularly to the tropical regions, where they thrive in abundant light and high humidity. Similar conditions suit them well in cultivation. Most cattleya orchids can tolerate a wide range of cultural conditions, however. Because of this and their ability to withstand some mistreatment, they are good choices for the novice.

Cattleya

Today the genus *Cattleya* contains more than 50 natural species and innumerable varieties. There are also thousands of hybrids developed by crossing other genera with *Cattleya.* Whatever their parentage, these hybrids all share the basic cultural requirements described here.

Cattleyas can be divided into two groups: the labiate or unifoliate forms, with a single leaf growing from each pseudobulb, and bifoliate cattleyas, with two or sometimes three leaves from each pseudobulb. Each stem of the unifoliate cattleyas bears two to six large flowers with showy lips. The bifoliate cattleyas have smaller but more abundant flowers with smallish lips and a thick, waxy texture.

The unifoliate cattleyas need the same growing conditions as the intergeneric hybrids. The bifoliate cattleyas need a slightly warmer temperature (60° to 65°) and a longer rest period. Until new growth starts, water these orchids sparingly.

Cattleyas are sun lovers, so a western or southern exposure suits them well. Plants will grow with other exposures, but bloom will be sparse.

Pot your cattleyas in osmunda or in fir bark (see page 10); fir bark is especially good for encouraging root growth in young plants. Because bloom tends to be more abundant when roots are confined, use relatively small pots for your cattleyas.

Ideal temperatures for cattleyas correspond to average home conditions—55° to 60° at night and 15° warmer by day. Plants will survive lower or higher temperatures, but they will not bloom abundantly. At lower temperatures growth is slow, and at higher temperatures growth is so rapid that plants become depleted. Most problems with cattleyas result from heat rather than cool weather. Plants can tolerate heat up to 95° for a few hours, but on very hot days be sure to mist plants frequently to lower the temperature. At the same time, keep the growing area well ventilated (see page 9).

Success with cattleyas depends largely upon watering practices. These plants like to dry out thoroughly between waterings. This doesn't mean that they don't like moisture, however. In summer, when the transpiration rate is high, they

Laelia Zip 'Fireball'

Epidendrum mariae 'Doris'

Sophrolaeliocattleya Paprika 'Tahiti'

Brassolaeliocattleya Crispin Rosales 'Crimson Pagoda'

Cattleya Forms

"Variety" is the word for orchids of the Cattleya group. Flower forms range from the spidery delicateness of *Epidendrum cochleatum* to the grand fullness of *Brassolaeliocattleya*.

Epidendrum cochleatum

Brassavola nodosa

Laelia purpurata carnea

**Broughtonia
sanguinea**

Epidendrum pseudepidendrum

Laelia flava aurantiaca 'Scarlet Gem'

Sophronitis rosea 'Darlene'

...Cattleya

Tantalizing colors—bright yellows, intense oranges, and deep purples—may spark your interest in these orchids. The colors from such orchids as the four pictured at the top of this page often carry into hybrids, such as the *Brassolaeliocattleya* below.

Brassolaeliocattleya Amenity 'Lemon Meadow'

need copious watering. In winter, keep plants barely moist, but not so dry that the pseudobulbs shrivel. When you water, always flood pots until excess water runs out the bottom.

To determine when to water plants, feel the osmunda fiber or push your fingers between the pot and the fir bark. If the potting material is springy and cool to the touch, it still holds enough water; but if it is crisp and woody, the plant needs watering again. Osmunda fiber holds water better than bark and stays moist longer. Plants in bark will therefore need more frequent watering than plants in osmunda.

Plants in osmunda need fertilizer only occasionally because the fibers contain some nutrients. One feeding a month in the summer and none at all during the rest of the year should be sufficient for osmunda-grown plants. Plants in fir bark, which is nearly devoid of nutrients, need fertilizing about twice a month during the spring and summer and once a month in the fall. Do not feed plants in winter when light intensity is low and plant growth is naturally slow.

C. aurantiaca (bifoliate) is often sold as an *Epidendrum*. This species has a slightly drooping spike of three or more heavy-textured, 2-inch flowers in yellow orange, orange, or red orange; some flowers may have dark brown or purple markings.

C. guttata (bifoliate) is a highly variable species with heavy-textured 2 to 4-inch flowers. The fragrant flowers, usually green with brown red to deep purple spots, have a white and rose lip. Each spike may have as many as 30 flowers in autumn.

C. labiata (labiate) is the most widely grown cattleya. The 7-inch flowers (even larger in some varieties) are rose or pink. The lip is rich magenta fading to rosy lilac on a ruffled margin. A pale yellow blotch, streaked with reddish purple, decorates the throat. Varieties ('Mossiae', 'Trianei', and 'Dowiana' are familiar examples) differ in flower size, color, and markings.

C. skinneri (bifoliate) is a popular, easy-blooming species. The 3½-inch flowers are entirely rose purple except for white in the throat; they develop in clusters of 4 to 12. Varieties include a pure white form and faintly fragrant types.

C. walkeriana (bifoliate), a dwarf species, produces one or two 3 to 5-inch flowers on short spikes. The fragrant, velvety flowers vary in color from bright rose purple to soft pinkish lilac; the lip is marked with bright amethyst and darker purple. *C. walkeriana* blooms irregularly, with most blooms in spring. It also requires much less water than other cattleyas during its rest period.

Epidendrum

This genus includes both epiphytic and terrestrial plants, most of which are easy to grow. Two groups of *Epidendrum* species occur, characterized by different types of pseudobulbs. Species with hard, round pseudobulbs are placed in the group Encyclia. *Encyclia* is often used as the genus name for orchids in this group. The other group, Euepidendrum, consists of softer-textured plants that have thin, stemlike pseudobulbs; these orchids are also known as reed-stem epidendrums.

The cultural requirements of epidendrums are basically similar to those of cattleya, though variations exist. The encyclia types do well in pots or baskets or on slabs if they are given a rest period after flowering. Reed-stem epidendrums perform best when planted in specially prepared beds outdoors; they need to be kept moist throughout the year.

Reed-stemmed types need an abundance of sun to flower but require cool roots. Mulch plants growing in the ground to keep the root area cool. Foliage will turn bright red and burn if the sun is too hot. At the other end of the scale, frost will burn tips at 28°, and plants will be killed to the ground at about 22°. In cold-winter areas, grow the reed-stemmed types in pots and move them indoors in winter. When blooms fade, cut the flowering stem back to within one or two joints of the ground.

All epidendrums grow well in fir bark or the other potting mixtures described on page 11. Those in bark will require a liquid fertilizer at every other watering; plants in other mixtures will need fertilizer monthly. In general, epidendrums prefer the same intermediate to warm temperatures given cattleyas (see page 32) with exceptions noted below.

E. atropurpureum, with short, globular pseudobulbs, grows to 16 inches. The 3-inch flowers are chocolate brown and pale green with lips of white and rose purple; 4 to 20 flowers bloom on each stem.

E. cochleatum has pear-shaped pseudobulbs with erect flower stems that bear 5 to 10 flowers, each 2 to 3 inches across. Flowers have narrow, twisted yellow green sepals and petals and a purplish black lip with lighter veins. Blooming season is irregular. Plants will withstand temperatures down to about 25°. *E. cochleatum* blooms all year.

E. ibaguense (*E. radicans*) produces erect, reed-like, leafy stems that reach 2 to 4 feet. On slender stems that rise well above the foliage, dense, globular clusters of 1 to 1½-inch red to yellow flowers appear at various times throughout the year. Many hybrids have flowers of other colors: pink, red violet, lavender, and white.

E. mariae reaches about 8 inches when in bloom. The 3-inch green flowers have broad white lips. *E. mariae* should be acclimated gradually to almost full sun. These orchids are best grown on a slab.

E. pseudepidendrum grows to 3½ feet. The 2½ to 3-inch flowers, apple green with a lip of brilliant orange or orange red, appear in clusters of three to five. This species prefers an intermediate temperature.

E. stamfordianum produces numerous tiny, fragrant yellow and red-spotted flowers in spring, on spikes that originate from the bases of all pseudobulbs. Plant grows to 30 inches.

Laelia

Closely related to cattleyas, these epiphytic orchids range from Mexico to South America. Generally, the plants have one or two evergreen leaves at the top of the pseudobulbs. Flowers resemble cattleyas but are usually smaller, with narrower petals. Culture is similar to that for cattleyas, but laelias should receive even more sun for best flowering. Between flowering and the start of new growth, laelias need very little water; during the rest of the year they should be allowed to dry out between waterings.

Several *Laelia* species are well suited to outdoor culture in areas where temperatures seldom dip below freezing; if winter temperatures are likely to go down to the mid-thirties, grow them in the most protected garden areas.

L. anceps has two to six rose violet flowers with purple-lined yellow throats, 2½ to 4 inches across, on each stem in fall and winter. Suitable for outdoor planting.

L. cinnabarina may have leaves and pseudobulbs flushed with purple. In spring and summer 2½-inch flowers appear, 5 to 15 on a stem; color is somewhat variable, but most common is bright cinnabar red.

L. flava develops four to eight 2½-inch flowers on each stem in spring or early summer. Flower color is variable, light orange yellow to vivid golden or butter yellow.

L. milleri, discovered in 1960, shows great promise in hybridization: a blood red form may easily give its rich color to crosses with *Cattleya*.

Flowers may be red orange or blood red, 4 to 10 on a spike.

L. purpurata has fragrant, 6 to 8-inch flowers, three to seven or more on each stem. Literally hundreds of varieties have been named; colors include almost pure white, white flushed and veined with pale amethyst purple, and pale amethyst purple with darker veins.

Brassavola

Brassavolas are very popular, easy-to-grow orchids recommended for the amateur. The most commonly know brassavola, *B. digbyana*, now goes by the genus name *Rhyncholaelia* (see listing below).

Culture is similar to that given cattleyas (see page 32). Brassavolas require abundant water and almost full sun while in active growth. When new pseudobulbs mature, withhold water for 2 weeks to allow a rest period. Erect brassavolas do well in pots; use baskets for the pendulous-stemmed species. In either case, drainage must be perfect. Do not divide brassavolas too frequently; allow them to become large, crowded specimens.

B. nodosa has an appealing nighttime fragrance that earned this orchid the nickname "Lady of the Night." This species is extremely variable in size, habit, and flower color. The plant's growth habit may be erect or pendulous; flowers range in size from 2 to 3½ inches across and in color from pale green or yellowish to almost pure white. A few named varieties are available. *B. nodosa* blooms throughout the year; it may be almost everblooming.

B. perrinii is also fragrant at night. The 2½ to 3-inch flowers appear in spring; they are yellow or greenish yellow with a pure white lip, sometimes spotted in the throat with apple green.

Rhyncholaelia

Native to the hot, dry regions of Mexico and Central America, rhyncholaelias are usually called brassavolas, the genus that formerly included them. They have been used extensively in the production of showy hybrids (see page 37).

Rhyncholaelias require the same growing conditions as cattleyas, but need less water; do not keep them overly moist at any time. Pot these orchids tightly in fir bark or tree fern fiber and give them a bright, sunny spot.

Rhyncholaelia digbyana is the popular species.

Its extremely fragrant, citrus-scented flowers appear in spring or summer. The petals and sepals are usually creamy white, flushed with green. The huge, deeply fringed lip is pale yellowish green, often with a deeper green area in the throat. *R. d. fimbripetala* has petals with fringed edges.

R. glauca is similar, although somewhat smaller and without a fringed flower.

Other Cattleya tribe members

Sophronitis coccinea is a small Brazilian orchid noted for its brilliant colors, from yellow through orange to crimson. It prefers a cool, shaded, humid spot in an intermediate greenhouse. Plant in a proportionately small, well-drained pot, using sphagnum moss and finely shredded tree fern fiber. Water frequently, with no rest period.

Caularthron (Diacrium) bicornutum has pure, sparkling white flowers that have earned the nickname "Virgin Orchid." With a lip faintly dotted with purple, the fragrant flowers crowd an erect stem with up to 20 buds. Culture is the same as for cattleyas. Feed heavily; do not divide too frequently.

Broughtonia sanguinea is showy: its 1-inch, cattleya-shaped flowers may vary in color but are usually a vivid crimson. The lip is yellowish or whitish with rose purple veins. Plant on a slab in almost full sun and keep on the dry side for almost continuous bloom. Broughtonia likes medium to warm temperatures, dislikes being disturbed.

Cattleya hybrids

Orchid hybridizers have crossed members of the cattleya group to produce extravagantly beautiful and diverse orchids. In fact, more hybrids are registered from this group than from any other in the orchid family. Familiar examples are the wonderful corsage orchids, hybrids usually involving *Cattleya*, *Laelia*, and *Rhyncholaelia*.

As if building an orchid from scratch, hybridizers bring together desirable characteristics from many orchids to form a single new flower. They often select the beautiful form and large size of the flowers of the genus *Cattleya*. The rich colors of *Laelia* show in many hybrids. *Rhyncholaelia digbyana* lends its frilled lip and green color to a host of modern orchids. And the vivid scarlet color of many new hybrids comes from *Sophronitis coccinea*.

The artificial genus *Laeliocattleya* was probably the first intergeneric hybrid (see page 21) produced. New versions of it are being developed to give us orchids in rich shades of yellow, orange, lavender, and even green. Although laeliocattleyas may not be as large as grand corsage orchids, their free-flowering habit and delicately shaped blooms make these orchids popular.

Brassocattleya is the name given to crosses involving *Cattleya* and *Rhyncholaelia* (*Rhyncholaelia*'s old name, *Brassavola*, is used in the resulting name). The characteristics of *Rhyncholaelia* stand out in these hybrids: flower colors suffused with green and full lips with various edgings, from subtle waviness to intricate frilliness. Frequently the citrus fragrance of *Rhyncholaelia* also passes on.

Laelia and *Rhyncholaelia* orchids are again combined with *Cattleya* forms to form the trigeneric hybrid genus *Brassolaeliocattleya*. Fortunately, this jawbreaker of a name is almost always shortened to BLC. The flower is full, like that of *Cattleya*. The lip is large and ruffled—a trait inherited from *Rhyncholaelia*. And the colors are those of *Laelia*: rich and bright. BLCs are the exotic hybrids that capture the attention of the beginning hobbyist and inspire the advanced grower.

Sophronitis, a newcomer to the hybridization scene, has been used to develop *Sophrolaeliocattleya* (shortened to SLC). This very popular group features intense colors, ranging from golden yellow through orange and orange red to vibrant red and red purple. A popular hybridizing trend with the SLCs is toward vivid scarlet coloration without yellow or purple undertones. SLCs do best in cool conditions.

By combining the best qualities of all four genera (*Cattleya*, *Laelia*, *Rhyncholaelia*, and *Sophronitis*), hybridizers have produced the quadrigeneric hybrid *Potinara*. An orchid combining the ideal qualities from each of the four is striking indeed, but because of genetic problems, few *Potinara* hybrids have been developed.

The genus *Epidendrum* shares its rich colors and free blooming quality in hybrids combining many members of the *Cattleya* tribe. *Epiphronitis* (from *Epidendrum* and *Sophronitis*), one of the earliest intergeneric crosses, dates from 1890. It is a charming, brightly colored orchid that still has appeal.

Two less important genera, *Caularthron* (under the synonymous name *Diacrium*) and *Broughtonia*, have also been used in crosses. The small size and bright color of *Broughtonia* shows in its crosses; *Caularthron* lends its delicate form and size to hybrid offspring.

Cymbidiums

Graceful plants lavish with bloom, cymbidiums are favorites in the home and the garden wherever nighttime temperatues fall to 60° or lower during the warmest months of the year. From February to early May, erect or arching spikes of flowers rise from long, narrow arching foliage. One spike may carry as many as 30 flowers, each 4 to 5 inches across, that can remain fresh and attractive for 8 weeks or more. Robust, mature plants may reach 3 to 5 feet high when in full bloom.

Today, most cymbidiums are hybrids of cool growing types. They will tolerate heat if necessary, but they must have cool night temperatures (45° to 55°) throughout the summer and early fall to set flower buds. Miniature cymbidiums will tolerate more heat than the large standard types, but they still prefer cool conditions.

From March to October, as new growth develops and matures, water plants copiously. At other times, keep the potting mix barely moist but never dry.

Give your cymbidiums enough light in summer and early fall to yellow the foliage (about 75 per cent of full sunlight). Don't worry about the sickly yellow appearance of the foliage, but do make certain that air circulation at this time is adequate. Once the flower buds begin to open, the plants should be shaded. Hybrids with pink or red flowers will have richer coloring if they are not shaded too heavily. Yellow or green-flowered hybrids, however, require heavy shading to prevent their colors from fading. Return your cymbidiums to the brighter light as soon as flowering is finished.

Many potting mixes are available for cymbidiums, from osmunda to fir bark to various mixtures of these with other organic materials. A good potting mixture for cymbidiums consists of 2 parts redwood bark, 2 parts peat moss, and 1 part sand. Another popular mix contains 2 parts each of fir bark, leaf mold, and peat moss, and 1 part sand. Packaged mixes designed specifically for cymbidiums are very satisfactory; they are the easiest approach if you have never grown these orchids. In any case, your mixture should drain fast yet retain moisture.

Cymbidiums need additional fertilizer. Give them a complete liquid fertilizer every 2 weeks from January through July; fertilize about once a month from August through December.

Do not disturb plants too often, because most cymbidiums bloom better when potbound. Repot them after blooming, but only when the pseudobulbs become crowded against the edges of their containers. Water lightly after repotting; when new growth becomes evident, increase moisture.

Of all the orchids suitable for outdoor culture, cymbidiums are the most widely grown. They will endure temperatures as low as 28° for a short time only; if a harder frost threatens, protect plants by covering them with polyethylene plastic. Flower spikes are more tender than other plant tissues. Cymbidiums planted outdoors also require protection from slugs and snails.

When you divide cymbidiums, keep a minimum of three healthy pseudobulbs (with foliage) in each division. Dust cuts with sulfur or paint them with tree seal to discourage rot.

Miniatures

For the cymbidium fancier who has limited space or lives in a climate that is too warm for conventional hybrids, the solution might be miniature cymbidiums. Because they bloom easily, produce many flowers, and have a compact growth habit, miniature cymbidiums are becoming popular. Many miniatures flower several months before the conventional cymbidiums, some as early as November.

Unlike conventional cymbidiums, miniatures do best when watered throughout most of the year. They can also stand hotter temperatures than the conventional type. In fact, miniature cymbidiums do well in an intermediate greenhouse (see page 8).

Hybrids

From a few species, growers have developed an amazing number of hybrids. A representative listing from the thousands of hybrids would be difficult to compile, but a few varieties should be mentioned because they are being used as parents in many crosses.

Cymbidium Alexanderi 'Westonbirt' is the most popular cymbidium parent. It contributes to its offspring such qualities as heavy foliage, slow growth, and sturdy, shapely rounded flowers. And, equally important, it produces consistently good hybrid offspring. Other hybrids that have proven their worth as parents include C. Balkis, C. Babylon 'Castle Hill', C. Rosanna 'Pinkie', and C. Nam Khan.

Cymbidium Voodoo 'Gypsy Red'

Cymbidium Starbright 'Cupella'

Cymbidium Parfait 'Monterey Hills'

Cymbidium

Cymbidiums offer a four-color selection. This page shows red, green, and white varieties; page 31, a tan variety. Above right is a miniature.

Cymbidium Seafoam 'Emerald'

Aerides tribe

Both beginners and advanced growers can find orchids to grow in this group. The Aerides tribe includes the easily grown house plant *Phalaenopsis*. For the more experienced grower, popular choices include *Doritis*, *Vanda*, and *Ascocentrum*, as well as their intergeneric crosses.

Orchids of this tribe color the tropical landscapes of Asia, Africa, and Australia. A greenhouse is the usual environment for Aerides orchids, although some can do well in the home or even outdoors in warm areas such as Florida and Hawaii.

Phalaenopsis

The name ''moth orchid'' suggests both the delicacy and grace of phalaenopsis flowers and the way they are carried on their stems. The sight of six to a dozen white flowers on a gracefully arching stem suggests a swarm of moths or butterflies in flight. Individual flowers last for two months or more, and the succession of blooms on a single plant may give you flowers for more than half the year.

Phalaenopsis orchids are native to the tropics of Asia, extending as far west as Africa and south to Australia. Their preferred temperature range—around 65° at night and 10° to 15° warmer during the day—is a very comfortable household environment. What the ordinary home does not supply (without special attention) is the preferred humidity: 60 to 70 per cent humidity pleases orchids but not the humans who live with them. The ideal humidity can most easily be provided in a greenhouse; but see page 8 for ways to increase humidity around orchids that you want to grow inside the home.

Phalaenopsis are relatively shade-loving plants, happiest with about half the light required by cattleyas. Although they can tolerate more light during fall and winter than during the summer months, they should not be subjected to direct sunlight.

Either fir bark or osmunda is a suitable potting material for phalaenopsis plants; see page 12 for potting techniques. Phalaenopsis differ from many other commonly grown orchids, however, in requiring repotting infrequently. Growth habit is monopodial (see page 6), which allows you to leave a plant undisturbed in its container until the potting mixture begins to break down and lose its open texture.

After the spring bloom or when new roots are forming at the base of the plant are the best times to repot a phalaenopsis. To repot, first prepare your potting material and container as described on page 12. Then remove the plant from the container in which it has been growing and clean off all old potting mixture. Below the ring of living roots, there is an inactive stub: break off the stub (or cut it off with a sterilized knife) and position the plant in the new container so that the bases of the leaves will be at the surface of the potting mixture. Trim live roots only as much as necessary to fit them into the pot. Potting mixture should be firmed around roots, but not as tightly as for cattleyas.

Because they have no pseudobulbs in which to store moisture, phalaenopsis plants should never be allowed to dry out completely. Like other orchids, they require good drainage and aeration, so be careful not to overwater. See page 9 for watering guidelines.

Phalaenopsis **Jane Almquist**

Phalaenopsis **Mellow Yellow**

Euanthe sanderiana 'Doris'

Phalaenopsis violacea 'Lee'

Phalaenopsis Layla Beard 'Show-Off'

The Exotic Aerides

For a vision of tropical paradise, grow an orchid from the Aerides tribe. Delicate forms and bright colors in contrasting combinations characterize this exotic group. You'll discover fragrance, too, as a bonus.

Rhynchostylis gigantea

Ascocenda Ophelia 'Papaya'

 Aerides group **41**

Ascocentrum curvifolium

Phalaenopsis Mad Hatter 'Tea Party'

...More Aerides

Though familiar moth orchids (upper right) still hold appeal, many orchid enthusiasts now grow some very different moth orchid relatives, including the varieties shown here and on page 41.

Vanda tricolor suavis

Vandanthe Rothschildiana 'Jessie'

Doritaenopsis Coral Gleam 'Samuel B. Mosher'

 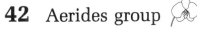

Especially during periods of active growth, phalaenopsis plants appreciate an application of liquid fertilizer with every other watering. In the less active growing season it is best not to fertilize.

Hybrids

More than 40,000 named hybrids have been developed within this genus. This large collection is grouped by color.

Whites. These sparkling flowers are white with small or faint markings, if any, on the lip.

Semi-albas. These flowers, also called whites-with-colored-lip, have the same pure white sepals and petals as the white hybrids, but the lip is colored with yellow, orange, red, or purple.

Pinks. Colors range from pale pink to rich purple, with or without a darker lip.

Candy stripes. White, pink, or golden flowers have faint to deep stripes in pink, purple, or brown. Stripes may cover the entire flower or appear only on its margins.

Sandy pinks. Gaining in popularity, the sandy pinks occur in varying pastel shades of brownish pink.

Yellows. Yellow greens to golds are the characteristic colors of this small rare group.

Novelties. This large group of dissimilar hybrids includes those bred from species parents rather than from combinations of selected hybrids. They have unusual colors and forms; most have contrasting markings. Parents that stand out from this group include varieties of *Phalaenopsis amboinensis*, *P. fuscata*, *P. gigantea*, *P. lueddemanniana*, *P. mariae*, *P. sumatrana*, and *P. violacea*.

Species

Phalaenopsis species are just beginning to gain popularity with amateur growers. Their greatest value is to commercial hybridizers, who use them to develop hybrids with richer colors, striking markings, and unusual forms.

P. amboinensis has 2 to 3-inch flowers, pale yellow with bars of cinnamon brown. It is used in producing yellow and novelty hybrids.

P. equestris (P. *rosea*) has a gracefully arching, many-flowered stem that produces flowers practically all year. The flowers, nearly 1 inch across, are pale rose red with a magenta rose lip marked in deep red. This species is sometimes used for creating miniature whites.

P. lueddemanniana has fragrant, long-lived flowers that vary in size and color; usually they are less then 2 inches in diameter and colored with brown, purple, and yellow, variously blotched and streaked. Several named varieties are commonly used in creating novelty hybrids.

P. mariae produces many yellow flowers marked with four transverse bars of chestnut brown; the lip is rose purple with white margins.

P. sumatrana has sturdy 2-inch flowers in creamy white barred with red brown; the lip is white marked with orange spots and purple streaks. Candy stripe hybrids may have P. *sumatrana* in their backgrounds.

P. violacea produces the most popular group of *Phalaenopsis* hybrids. Its 2 to 3-inch flowers are quite variable in color, typically greenish white with a bright violet purple blotch on the base of each sepal and petal; the lip is golden yellow with purple markings.

Vanda

Originally from the Philippines, Malaysia, and the Himalayas, these are now grown extensively as a commercial crop in the Hawaiian Islands. Growth habit is monopodial (see page 6); some types eventually reach 4 feet or more. Because aerial roots form along the stems, the top portion of the plant may be cut off and rooted to make a plant of more manageable size. The old portion of the plant may then produce offshoots which can be removed and potted after they form roots.

Vanda species and hybrids fall into two groups by leaf type, only one of which is suited to temperate conditions. Terete-leafed plants (those with pencil-like leaves) require so much light to flower that they must be grown in full sun. But because they must also have night temperatures above 50°, they are suitable only in tropical countries or unshaded, well-ventilated greenhouses with tropical temperatures. Vandas with strap-shaped leaves require less light and so may be flowered successfully outside the tropics. Hybrids of the two leaf types (called semi-terete) also have the exceptionally high light requirement; when these hybrids are crossed back to strap-leafed species, however, the resulting hybrids generally need no more light than the original strap-leafed forms.

All vandas appreciate plenty of water but require perfect drainage; they demand good air circulation and enjoy somewhat more humidity than is comfortable for humans. Where summer temperatures always remain above 50°, vandas benefit from being moved outdoors during this period. Such a move should be gradual to accustom the plant to the brighter light outdoors (see page 29). Fertilize vandas once a week during the growing season with a diluted solution of a complete fertilizer.

There are many hybrids within the genus *Vanda*. Of these, the following list represents those that have proven themselves outstanding performers in growth and flowering: *Vandanthe* (*Euanthe* bred with true *Vanda*) Rothchildiana, blue; *V.* Eisenhower, tan to yellow; *V.* Nellie Morley, rich pink.

V. coerulea produces large 3 to 4-inch flowers, varying from pale blue to dark blue, on 1 to 2-foot stalks in late summer or fall. Strap leaves are 6 to 10 inches long. *V. coerulea* can be grown either in a bright, cool spot in an intermediate greenhouse or with cool orchids.

V. sanderiana is still listed here under the genus *Vanda*, although its preferred genus is now *Euanthe*. This recent change has caused some confusion, particularly with regard to *Vanda* hybrids (see above). *V. sanderiana* grows to 3 feet; beautiful, flat 3 to 4-inch flowers in fall combine white, rose, greenish yellow, brown, and dark red.

V. teres is a terete-leafed species of great value in the tropical flower trade. Plant grows to 7 feet; flowers are white and deep rose, 3 to 4 inches across, on stalks of two to five blooms in late spring and summer.

V. tricolor suavis grows to 3 feet. Sweetly fragrant flowers are white spotted with red purple, to 3 inches across. Flowering season is winter.

Aerides

Tropical Asia is the native home of these epiphytic orchids, some of which are very tall. Lacking pseudobulbs, the plants have a central stem with fleshy green leaves. In summer, graceful pendent spikes carry many closely set, fragrant flowers of waxy texture.

Cultural requirements of aerides are much like those of vandas. Aerides do well in baskets, which allow for expansion of the rampant, brittle roots and for display of the pendent flower spikes. Water copiously in spring and summer, but not so much the rest of the year. Grow in bright light. Fertilize regularly and repot infrequently.

A. lawrenceae produces sprays of 15 to 20 sweetly scented flowers in late summer and early fall. Color is greenish white tipped with purple; a pure white form is also available.

A. multiflorum has 1-inch, white and purple flowers in summer. These are carried in great numbers on stalks longer than the 9-inch, straplike leaves. Needs sun and even moisture all year.

A. odoratum grows to 5 feet and gives numerous 1-inch white flowers blotched with purple. Its spicy fragrance alone would be reason enough to grow this species.

Other Aerides tribe members

Phalaenopsis and Vanda have many beautiful cousins. Those listed here should be easy to find; specialty catalogs will offer many more.

Angraecum
From Africa, Malagasy and adjacent islands come several fine epiphytic plants that bloom in winter. They have lovely starlike white or greenish white flowers with long curved spurs. Keep plants moist all year except in fall; then allow them to dry out between waterings. Grow in diffused light. They may be grown with cattleyas.

A. eburneum bears eight or more 3-inch, waxy greenish white blooms alternately on stems longer than the 9-inch, arching, strap-shaped leaves. Plant may reach 6 feet.

A. sesquipedale grows to 36 inches, bearing fragrant, 6-inch ivory white flowers, each with a 10-inch spur. Likes cool (55°) nights.

Ascocentrum
This small group, composed mostly of epiphytic orchids, ranges from southern China, Taiwan, and the Philippines to Java and Borneo. Plants have leathery leaves; short, erect spikes of small flowers bloom in late spring and early summer, as many as 50 to a stem. Ascocentrums require the same culture as vandas.

A. curvifolium, with stems to 6 inches, has ½-inch flowers that are variable in color, ranging from purple through rich rusty red to orange. *A. miniatum* is similar to *A. curvifolium* but somewhat taller, with 1-inch flowers colored brilliant yellow orange, orange, or orange red.

Doritis pulcherrima
This variable orchid, used extensively in hybridization, is native from Burma to Sumatra. Stems reach 6 inches and produce spikes of ½ to 2-inch flowers during a long period in autumn and winter. Flowers are usually pale rose purple, although some are nearly white, with a darker lip. The form *buyssoniana* has larger, more richly colored flowers.

Rhynchostylis
Native to the Philippines and India, these epiphytic orchids have small, colorful flowers tightly

packed on long pendent stems; hence their common name, "foxtail orchid." Foliage is leathery and straplike growing in a fan shape; growth habit is monopodial. Plants resent being disturbed when replanting is necessary. At that time, remove as much old potting mix as you can without taking the plant out of its container; then gently fill in around roots with fresh material. Culture is similar to that for vandas.

R. gigantea grows to 28 inches; pendent "tails" of hundreds of waxy, 1-inch white flowers spotted with red appear in autumn or early winter. Flowers are highly fragrant.

R. retusa blooms in summer and autumn; pendent 2-foot spikes carry many fragrant white flowers spotted purple, each about ¾ inch across. Plants may reach 12 inches.

Aerides hybrids

Along with its countless species and hybrids, the Aerides tribe offers hundreds of intergeneric crosses. Hybridizing has developed richly colored flowers, better blooming plants, and delightful miniatures.

Hybridizers have brought together desirable characteristics from many genera to form this collection of extremely showy hybrids. Bright colors are derived from *Doritis, Ascocentrum,* and *Renanthera. Aerides* and *Rhynchostylis* contribute to the hybrids an ability to produce large, dense flower clusters. The small flower size of these orchids is given a boost by introducing such large flowered genera as *Vanda, Euanthe,* and *Phalaenopsis.* Dwarf hybrids are created with *Ascocentrum, Doritis,* and *Saccolabium.*

The predominant genus used for hybridization is *Vanda.* Because it is compatible with a large number of its relatives, *Vanda* has produced an amazing number of intergeneric hybrid orchids. *Vanda* is crossed with *Phalaenopsis* to produce *Vandaenopsis,* a hybrid genus that combines the characteristics of whichever species are used as parents. *Vanda* and *Euanthe* together produce the popular hybrid genus *Vandanthe* (see page 44).

The charming *Ascocendas* result from crossing a *Vanda* with an *Ascocentrum.* These "miniature vandas" retain the dwarf stature of the ascocentrum parent and bear flowers whose brilliance surpasses that of vanda; blooms frequently.

Vanda has also been combined with *Renanthera,* a genus of large vandalike orchids with spider-shaped scarlet, orange, or crimson blooms. The flowers of the resulting *Renantanda* hybrids have the rich color of *Renanthera* but show the fuller form of *Vanda.*

The second most commonly used parent, *Phalaenopsis,* has produced a large share of hybrids. "Moth orchids" have been bred with *Renanthera* (giving rise to *Renanthopsis*), *Aerides* (producing *Aeridopsis*), and *Arachnis* (giving rise to *Arachnopsis*). *Phalaenopsis* combines with the dark-flowered forms of *Doritis* to produce *Doritaenopsis,* a hybrid much like a miniature phalaenopsis with beautifully proportioned, rich pink or red flowers.

Conserving Native American Orchids

As new cities sprang up and others expanded, the boundaries of the wild areas shrank and along with them the wild orchid populations. Also endangering these populations were the commercial and amateur collectors who usually obtained specimens by digging them from their native ground—a practice that is no longer considered acceptable.

Popular native genera include *Calypso, Calopogon, Cypripedium* (not *Paphiopedilum*), *Epipactis,* and *Habenaria.* Though many species of these and other genera are still common in nature, those that are threatened with extinction are the very ones most in demand. Where areas are destined for destruction by other means, however, collecting is welcomed.

These orchids are also among the most difficult to transplant into a greenhouse or garden. In nature they often survive with the help of a soil fungus—a situation not easily matched in cultivation. Many require extremely acid or alkaline soil; some require perfect drainage while others do best in boggy conditions; and many won't grow without freezing temperatures during dormancy.

Cultivation of these orchids is recommended to the experienced grower only. If you are in this category, purchase plants from dealers who raise their own seedlings or divisions. These plants, having been adapted to garden conditions, may even do better than collected specimens.

Dendrobium tribe

With about 1,500 species native to India, Burma, Ceylon, China, Japan, and Australia as well as several hundred hybrids, this is the second largest group of orchids (the Cattleya group is the largest). Because of their wide distribution and their structural diversity, dendrobiums show considerable variety in their cultural requirements. Dendrobium species fall into one of the following six classes according to their growing habits.

1. Deciduous species that require a cool, dry rest period. During the months of active growth, give these orchids cattleya temperatures (see page 32) and abundant water. When foliage matures (one immature leaf falls off, leaving a solitary leaf) reduce watering for 6 to 8 weeks, giving the plant only enough water to prevent shriveling of the canes. When the leaves fall, keep plants in a bright, cool spot (45° to 50° nighttime temperature). When flower buds start to show, move plants back to warmth and resume watering. The species *Dendrobium chrysanthum*, *D. nobile*, and *D. wardianum* belong in this category.

2. Deciduous species that require a warm, dry rest period are also grown under cattleya conditions during the period of active growth. When foliage matures reduce the amount of water given, but continue the cattleya temperature. This group includes the species *D. parishii* and *D. pierardii*.

3. Evergreen species that need a cool, moist rest period. Grow these under cattleya conditions until foliage matures in the fall. Then move them to a cool spot (50° at night), but continue to water often enough to prevent drying. When new growth starts, move them back to the cattleya temperature range. Species in this group are *D. chrysotoxum*, *D. densiflorum*, *D. farmeri*, *D. fimbriatum*, *D. moschatum*, and *D. thyrsiflorum*.

4. "Black-haired" evergreen species require moderately cool temperatures all year. They are best grown on the cool side of an intermediate greenhouse (page 8); water them like cattleyas (page 32). When foliage matures allow a short, dry rest period. The black-haired species include *D. dearei*, *D. formosum*, and *D. infundibulum*.

5. "Antelope" evergreen species prefer warm temperatures all year. Grow this group with cattleyas, but give them the brightest spot in the greenhouse. Water them as you would the cattleyas, but without a rest period. The species *D. gouldii* and *D. stratiotes* represent the antelope types.

6. Evergreen species that need warm temperatures all year, with a slight reduction in water during a rest period. Grow these dendrobiums with cattleyas and give them abundant water while in active growth. Water less frequently when foliage matures. Resume normal watering during flowering. After flowering, restrict water again until new growth is well along. The popular species *D. bigibbum*, its even more popular form *phalaenopsis*, and the natural hybrid *D. superbiens*, are members of this group.

The following list contains descriptions of some common species of this large and varied group of orchids.

D. aggregatum grows to 10 inches and produces small vivid yellow, sweetly scented flowers in spring. Its form *jenkinsii* is even smaller: a real miniature.

D. bigibbum phalaenopsis grows to 24 inches. Its 3½-inch flowers, shaped much like *Phalaenopsis* blooms, vary from pure white to deep rose or purple with a darker lip. Blooms appear in fall.

D. chrysotoxum reaches 20 inches, bears drooping spikes of fragrant 2-inch, golden yellow flowers in spring. Blooms come from old pseudobulbs as well as new.

D. densiflorum develops up to 15 inches. Short-lived, 2-inch flowers appear in spring or summer; they are delicately fragrant, bright butter yellow with a hairy, orange yellow lip.

D. formosum has black-haired stems to 18 inches; flowers appear in the fall, 3 to 4 inches across, pure white except for a yellow throat. The form *giganteum* has 5-inch flowers.

D. gouldii grows to 4 feet or more and produces 2-foot, many-flowered spikes in fall. Yellowish flowers have purple and brown markings.

D. nobile grows to 40 inches; its 2-inch white flowers, tipped with rose purple, have a crimson blotch on the throat. Blooms in winter and spring. *D. nobile* has many named varieties.

D. parishii grows to 24 inches high. The 2-inch, rhubarb-scented flowers appear in spring and summer; each is usually rose-purple with a lighter, downy lip that is blotched deep purple on each side of the throat.

D. pierardii reaches 30 inches; pendent flowering stems appear in spring; pink blooms or white ones flushed with pink, have lips of yellow with purple stripes.

Dendrobium American Beauty 'Roya'

Dendrobium

Free-blooming dendrobiums aren't as fragile as they look. As cut flowers they last well and add elegance to any arrangement. Popular types include moth-orchidlike hybrids (above) and drooping cluster types (right). Or you can choose from the many other kinds on page 46.

Dendrobium aggregatum '**Papaya**'

Dendrobium nobile 'Oroville'

Dendrobium bigibbum phalaenopsis 'Petite'

 # Odontoglossum tribe

The Odontoglossum tribe is one of the largest and most varied in the orchid family. Long popular with orchid growers because of their easy culture and free-flowering habit, the members of this tribe have gained interest recently because of their cool temperature requirements—a definite advantage in this period of soaring fuel costs.

The native environment of these orchids extends over tropical America from Mexico to Bolivia, from the coast to the heights of the Andes. Most are well suited to indoor growing. The oncidiums are the most adaptable and tolerate the home environment best, but odontoglossums and miltonias also do well if given cool temperatures.

Odontoglossum

Delicate colors and ruffled edges characterize the blooms of these epiphytic orchids; predominant colors are white, yellow, brown, and pink. Plants generally have flattened pseudobulbs, each sheathed with small leaves and having two leaves at the top.

Most odontoglossums prefer cool conditions, since the native habitats of most species are foggy regions high in the Andes Mountains of South America. Night temperatures of 45° to 50° in winter and daytime readings in the low to midseventies are satisfactory; keep daytime temperatures as low as possible, especially in summer—below 80° if you can.

Some popular odontoglossums, including *O. crispum* and *O. luteo-purpureum*, require very cool conditions: a daytime temperature of 60° is the maximum. Though these cooler types are most easily grown in the Pacific Northwest, they will grow wherever cool temperatures can be provided.

In warm areas, choose from the many species that do not have restrictive temperature requirements: *O. harryanum*, *O. rossii*, and *O. uroskinneri* perform satisfactorily when grown with cymbidiums; and *O. grande*, *O. pendulum*, *O. pulchellum* can be grown in cattleya conditions (see pages 32–33), provided the summer nights stay at or below 60°. *O. pendulum* and *O. pulchellum* require a little less light than cattleyas.

Transplant after flowering in fall or in early spring, but never in hot summer weather. Plants thrive in crowded conditions, so use small pots relative to the size of the plants.

Odontoglossums appreciate plenty of light as long as heat is low, but no direct sun. They require constant high humidity (about 70 per cent) and water throughout the year.

O. crispum has 2½ to 3-inch flowers, most commonly pale rose with fringed edges, but frequently flushed pink dotted with brown or reddish brown. Pendent flower stems usually appear in spring or summer, although the blooming season may vary. This species has more than 100 named varieties.

O. grande, called the tiger orchid, produces three to seven 6-inch yellow flowers barred with reddish brown on each foot-long stalk. Blooming season is fall.

O. harryanum grows to 20 inches; wavy 3-inch, chestnut brown flowers are diversely marked with yellow, white, and purple. Flowers appear in summer or early fall.

(Continued on page 51)

Oncidium pusillum

Miltonia Hanover 'Lincoln'

The Fanciful Odontoglossum

"Spider," "pansy," "dancing dolls," and other fanciful names are given to the orchids of the Odontoglossum tribe. They're fascinating flowers—diverse in color, shape, and size. The variety in the genus *Oncidium* (left) alone will intrigue you. Differences in flower forms stand out when you compare the full, rounded *Miltonia* (below) with the elongated, spidery *Brassia* (bottom).

Clockwise from top: *Oncidium cabagre, O. harrisonianum, O. longipes, O.* Dainty *(pulchellum x cheirophorum), O. andigenum.*

Miltonia Eldridge Sabourin 'Bridal Veil'

Brassia verrucosa

Oncidium macranthum

Odontoglossum Kopan 'Easter'

Odontonia Marin

Colmanara Sir Jeremiah 'Lilian'

Miltassia Gordon Dillon

...Odontoglossum

If you want something new and different, consider Odontoglossums, which offer a grand selection of hybrids. Each hybrid's name is made up of parts of its parents' names: *Miltassia*, for example, is *Miltonia* combined with *Brassia*. *Colmanara* is a completely new name for hybrids developed from *Miltonia*, *Oncidium*, and *Odontoglossum*.

Odontocidium Crowborough 'Pixie'

Odontioda Ecuyer 'Burgundy'

O. luteo-purpureum has many named varieties; 3 to 4-inch flowers are brilliant purplish brown marked with yellow. The fringed lip is pale yellow with rose to purplish brown spots. Blooms in winter or spring.

O. nobile produces up to 100 blooms on each stem in spring. Faintly fragrant 2½ to 3-inch flowers vary in color from white to flushed pink, with the lip spotted and streaked in rose and crimson.

O. pendulum (*O. citrosmum*) bears drooping sprays of fragrant, long-lived flowers in late spring. Flowers vary in color but are typically white, lightly flushed or dotted with pink, with the lip bright or pale violet.

O. pulchellum, a small plant that reaches 10 inches, is easy to grow but not especially showy. The 1 to 2-inch waxy white flowers, produced in spring, have a lily-of-the-valley fragrance.

O. rossii is a winter-flowering species that bears clusters of three to five white, yellow, or blush pink flowers, flushed and spotted with dark brown. Each bloom is 2 to 3 inches across.

O. uro-skinneri reaches 30 inches; each large stem may carry as many as twenty 1-inch green and brown flowers with lavender lips. Blooms appear in early spring.

Oncidium

Members of this large group of epiphytic orchids, native to Mexico and Central and South America, produce long spikes of beautiful yellow flowers variously marked with brown. Some species have compressed pseudobulbs topped by one or two fleshy leaves; others are almost without bulbs; and still others have pencil-like leaves. Flowers may be small and numerous or large and sparse, depending on the individual species.

Growing conditions for cattleyas (see page 32) are generally satisfactory for oncidiums. Species native to higher and cooler elevations (*O. tigrinum, O. macranthum*) prefer cool temperatures as cymbidiums or odontoglossums do. All oncidiums appreciate considerable sunlight, but some shade is beneficial when they are flowering. They require abundant water throughout the growing and flowering season and a dry period with no water for several weeks following completion of new growth.

O. ampliatum, called the turtle orchid because of the shape of its pseudobulbs, grows to 30 inches. In spring, a mature plant may have hundreds of red-spotted yellow flowers on each stem.

O. cheirophorum is a charming miniature that grows to 6 inches. In fall, fragrant, ¼-inch yellow flowers with green sepals bloom in dense, branched clusters. Grows well under artificial light.

O. crispum reaches 1 to 1½ feet; throughout the year, shiny brown, 1½ to 3-inch flowers with yellow and red at base of petals and sepals are borne in profusion on arching stems. Never let plant dry out completely. It grows well in hanging containers. Many named varieties are available.

O. kramerianum is much like *O. papilio* except that it does not flower so freely; its top sepal and petals are shorter; and the lower sepals are spotted, rather than banded, with brown.

O. macranthum has very long, vining flower spikes that produce ruffled 4-inch flowers in summer. Flower color is yellow flushed with brown; the lip is yellow, white, and purple.

O. papilio can reach 3 feet when in bloom. Produced at any time of year, flowers are 4 to 5 inches long and 2½ inches across; 2 to 3-foot flower stems continue to produce buds for several years. The top sepal and petals are brown with bands of yellow; lower sepals and petals curve downward around the brown-edged yellow lip. *O. papilio* grows well in artificial light.

O. pusillum is a miniature that blooms continually with 1-inch flowers in bright yellow barred with reddish brown. It grows best on a slab where it can dry out between waterings; it does well in artificial light.

O. sphacelatum yields sprays of more than 200 brown-spotted, 1-inch yellow flowers in winter and spring.

O. splendidum grows to 3 feet and produces numerous 3-inch flowers in winter. Flower color is yellow green, barred and spotted with red brown; the lip is yellow. It prefers full sun.

O. triquetrum bears stems of 1-inch green and purple flowers in fall. Each stem may carry up to a dozen blooms. It grows well under artificial light.

Miltonia

Native of Costa Rica to Colombia and Brazil, the miltonias are called pansy orchids because their flat-faced, open flowers resemble pansies in shape and markings. These epiphytic orchids have elongated pseudobulbs with long, graceful light green leaves that may produce a clump of foliage a foot or more in diameter.

Light requirements divide miltonias into two groups. Members of one group, including the Colombian and Panamanian species and their hybrids, grow best under the light conditions paphiopedilums require (see page 54). The second group includes the Brazilian species and hybrids, which require light conditions similar to cattleyas (see page 32).

All miltonias require cool nights to flower: cattleya temperatures of 55° to 60° are satisfactory. They will tolerate daytime heat to 90° for short periods, but it's best to keep temperatures below 80°.

Keep miltonias moist except during dull gray periods in winter; decrease the frequency of watering at that time to prevent rotting. Humidity should be moderately high; 60 per cent is ideal, but an acceptable range is 50 to 70 per cent.

Miltonias flower best when potbound. Repot every year or two to allow your plants to reach mature size. Repot in small fir bark when new growth starts, in cool weather if possible. Fertilize miltonias once a month during the growing season, but not at all in winter.

Of the twenty or so species of *Miltonia*, *M. roezlii* and *M. vexillaria* have been used extensively to produce hybrids. The many varieties of these two species have been used to create striking, large-flowered hybrids, including the popular *Miltonia* Bleuana. These hybrids vary in color from pure white to deep crimson and flower at various times of the year.

M. clowesii (Brazil) produces flower spikes to 2 feet in the fall; 2 to 3-inch flowers are chestnut brown, barred and tipped with yellow. The lip has a distinctive fiddle shape and is half white, half purple.

M. regnelli (Brazil) has 3-inch white flowers suffused with rose purple at the base of petals; the light pink lip is edged with white. In fall each stem produces three to five flowers. Plant grows to 12 inches.

M. roezlii (Panama, Colombia) blooms in winter and spring. Flowers are velvety white with a purple blotch at the base of each petal; the lip is purplish white with a yellow base.

M. spectabilis (Brazil) reaches 20 inches; blooms in summer. Flowers have large, creamy white sepals and petals, and a broad rose purple lip.

M. vexillaria (Colombia) has soft, grayish green foliage to 20 inches. Each upright stem bears up to a dozen flowers (to 4 inches across), usually in some shade of pink to red with a darker lip.

M. warscewiczii (Panama, Colombia) produces dense, many-flowered spikes in spring. Fragrant, 2-inch flowers vary from brownish red to yellow; the lip is rose purple, marked with brownish red and edged with white.

Brassia

Found from Mexico south to Brazil and Peru, this group of large epiphytic plants features evergreen leaves rising from plump pseudobulbs. Flower spikes, generally elongated and pendent, carry many blooms with long, slender petals and sepals. Brassia's common name, spider orchid, comes from these elongated flower parts. Almost all brassias are fragrant, especially on warm days.

Culture is similar to that given cattleyas (see page 32). Give brassias a fairly sunny spot, with warmth and moisture throughout the year. After new growth matures, give them a dry rest period of about 2 weeks. Pot brassias in tightly packed osmunda or shredded tree fern fiber, or mount them firmly on tree fern slabs.

B. caudata has flower spikes that may reach 1½ feet and produce 3 to 12 flowers. Flowers, 5 to 8 inches long, may be yellowish, yellow green, or greenish, spotted or blotched with light or dark brown; the lip has fuzzy ridges. This autumn to early winter bloomer may flower twice a year.

B. gireoudiana produces flowers more than 12 inches long in late spring and early summer. Flower color is greenish yellow, blotched with very dark or almost blackish brown; the lip is pale yellow marked with brown.

B. longissima has spidery flowers that occasionally measure 21 inches long. Flowers are yellow to greenish yellow, with the bases of the sepals and petals marked in reddish brown; the pale yellow lip is spotted and blotched with brown.

B. verrucosa, a spring and early summer bloomer, has flower spikes up to 2 feet long. Eight-inch, pale green flowers are spotted with dark green or red; the whitish lip is spotted with red and very dark green.

Other Odontoglossum tribe members

Technically, these orchids do not belong in the Odontoglossum tribe, but they are listed here because they have been hybridized with true members of this tribe.

Cochlioda
These colorful, odontoglossumlike orchids are native to the Andean regions of South America. Flowers in brilliant shades of rose, red, and red orange decorate gracefully arching sprays. *C. noetzliana* has 2-inch, bright red orange flowers; the lip has a yellow spot. Grow these summer

bloomers like the cool odontoglossums (see page 48).

Rodriguezia
These small, easily grown plants come from northern South America. R. secunda bears short sprays of twenty to thirty 1-inch flowers, varying from almost pure white through several shades of pink to brilliant rose red; it often blooms more than once a year. R. venusta has slightly larger, very fragrant flowers in white tinged with pink; the lip is marked with yellow. R. venusta usually blooms in autumn but may bloom at any time. Culture of rodriguezias is similar to that given cattleyas (see page 32), but no rest period is required.

Trichocentrum
These attractive, compact plants are native from Mexico to southern Brazil. Easily grown, they are profuse, dependable bloomers. The proportionately large flowers are brightly colored. T. albo-coccineum blooms in late summer and autumn, producing long-lived 2-inch flowers that vary in color, usually greenish outside and maroon brown inside; the large lip is white with a purple blotch. Trichocentrums do best in small pots with good drainage. A combination of chopped sphagnum and shredded tree fern fiber makes a fast-draining potting mix. Do not repot too frequently; about once every other year. Give these orchids abundant water throughout the year. They also require high humidity, moderately bright light, and intermediate to warm temperatures.

Trichopilia
Ranging from Mexico to Brazil, the epiphytic Trichopilia species have large, cattleyalike flowers, one to four on each stem. T. suavis has creamy white 4-inch flowers; the trumpet-shaped lip is the same color, but heavily fluted and spotted with pink. Early spring is the blooming season. T. tortilis grows to 12 inches and blooms in spring or fall. Flowers have narrow, twisted sepals and brownish purple or rosy lavender petals; the lip is white, spotted with red or brown. Trichopilias require the same care as oncidiums: ample water during the growing season, followed by a 2 to 3-week rest period; a temperature range comfortable for the home; and some sunlight.

Intergeneric hybrids
Dozens of hybrid genera have been developed within the Odontoglossum tribe. The genera Odontoglossum, Oncidium, and Miltonia provide parents for many crosses, but hybrids have also been developed from less well-known genera such as Cochlioda, Rodriguezia, and Trichocentrum. Some of these intergeneric hybrids have large, beautiful flowers; others have flowers that are striking or unusual.

The genus Oncidium lends its free-blooming habit and vigor to many hybrids. Hybrids with a prominent lip usually have oncidiums or miltonias (or both) in their backgrounds. Miltonias and odontoglossums contribute to the development of large-flowered hybrids. Odontoglossums featuring broad petals and sepals are often crossed with oncidiums to compensate for the latter's usually small petals and sepals.

The color range of hybrids is wide: rich, earthy tones come from oncidiums and odontoglossums; miltonias give their soft, velvety hues; and bright colors come from cochliodas, rodriguezias, and trichocentrums. Dwarf hybrids have been developed from such compact-growing genera as Cochlioda and Rodriguezia and the small species of Oncidium. The genus Brassia gives rise to curiously elongated flower parts.

Because the cool temperature requirements of many Odontoglossum tribe members have limited their popularity, hybridizers have crossed these orchids with warm-growing kinds. The resulting hybrids do well with intermediate temperatures.

Hybrids that involve Miltonia and Oncidium are given the name Miltonidium; they have the small flower size, rich coloring, and warm temperature preference of Oncidium but the extremely large lip of Miltonia. The hybrid genus Odontocidium combines Odontoglossum and Oncidium; the good-size flowers are borne on large sprays.

Odontobrassia and Brassidium result from crossing Brassia with Odontoglossum and Oncidium, respectively. Both hybrid genera have the spidery flower parts characteristic of Brassia. The flowers of Odontobrassia are the larger, but those of Brassidium occur in large sprays.

Some very popular hybrids have the genus Cochlioda in their parentage. Combined with Odontoglossum, Cochlioda gives rise to Odontioda, a series of hybrids with full, rounded flowers in bright reddish colors. Crossing Odontioda with Miltonia creates the genus Vuylstekeara; these are large-lipped versions of Odontioda. Combined with Oncidium, Odontioda gives rise to Wilsonara, a hybrid genus featuring many-flowered spikes of star-shaped blooms in shades of reddish brown and yellow.

Cypripedium tribe

The Cypripedium tribe is the most primitive evolutionary group in the orchid family. These orchids are called lady's slippers because their lip is shaped like a pouch or the toe of a slipper.

The orchids of the Cypripedium tribe are primarily terrestrial. Widespread in their distribution, they range over Europe, Asia, and North and South America. Members of the genus *Paphiopedilum* are found in southern Asia, in habitats ranging from hot jungles to cool mountain peaks. Orchids of the genus *Cypripedium* inhabit the temperate regions of Asia, Europe, and North America. *Phragmipedium* species are native to South America and southern Mexico.

Paphiopedilum

These lovely lady's slipper orchids flower in striking, often bizarre, color combinations: background colors may be white, yellow, green, or a combination, with markings in tan, mahogany brown, maroon, green, or white. With their lacquered or waxy textures, these flowers sometimes appear more artificial than real. You will almost always find lady's slippers sold as cypripediums, but the vast majority are species or hybrids of *Paphiopedilum*.

Paphiopedilums fall into two broad categories: those native to the high mountains where the climate is cool and moist, and those that dwell on warm forest floors. Members of the first group have grassy green foliage; those in the second group have mottled leaves. Most of the green-leafed forms produce flowers in winter, and the mottled-leafed forms usually flower in summer; some species, however, bloom off and on throughout the year. A robust, mature plant from either group can bear as many as 30 flowers at once.

Different kinds of culture are necessary for the two groups of paphiopedilums. Green-leafed plants are cool growing, requiring temperatures of 50° to 55° at night and about 70° during the day. In hot summer weather, try to keep heat down by misting or shading plants. These species will not flower unless the nighttime temperature from mid-March to mid-June is consistantly 60° or less.

Species in the second group, recognized by their mottled foliage, need temperatures of 60° to 65° at night and 70° to 85° during the day. They will tolerate more summer heat than the green-leafed types.

Hybrids representing crosses between these two types grow best under intermediate temperatures: about 60° at night and 80° during the day. Since paphiopedilums are tolerant of extremes, most of these temperature ranges are flexible.

Unlike cattleyas, which require almost full sun, paphiopedilums prefer dappled to bright light without direct sunshine. Inadequate sunlight turns the leaves a deep green color; excessive sunlight causes pale green leaves; and extreme sun scorches leaves and quickly desiccates plants.

These orchids grow continuously. Since they have no pseudobulbs in which to store moisture for use during dry spells, paphiopedilums require an even level of moisture all year. Water your paphiopedilums every 3 to 5 days during sunny weather, and once a week or less during dull, gray weather or rest periods. As with all orchids, water plants thoroughly until excess water runs out the bottom of the container. This will leach out salts that might otherwise accumulate and injure roots.

Although paphiopedilums are basically terrestrial, they can be grown in shredded osmunda or in medium grade fir bark, with or without crushed dried oak leaves. Repot each year after bloom; divide large plants, keeping three growing centers to a container. Do not pot paphiopedilums as tightly as you would cattleyas, but be sure that the potting mix is well settled in the pot. After repotting, water plants only enough to keep the mix barely moist. When new growth begins (in about 3 weeks) start regular watering. Do not allow water to remain in leaf joints; this may encourage a bacterial rot (see page 15).

Give paphiopedilums moderate humidity (30 to 50 per cent) and maintain good air circulation (see page 9). No fertilizing is necessary if paphiopedilums are potted in osmunda. If you grow them in fir bark, weak monthly applications of fertilizer may be necessary throughout spring and summer. Paphiopedilum roots are extremely sensitive to fertilizers, so dilute the mixture more than the directions specify.

Species

Here are a few *Paphiopedilum* species that are easy to find. Because of the trend toward growing more species orchids, you should be able to find other species as well at specialty nurseries.

P. barbatum has leaves mottled with dark

(Continued on page 56)

Paphiopedilum Maudiae 'Stella'

Paphiopedilum

One of the four most popular orchid groups, paphiopedilums are often called cypripediums. Hybrid paphiopedilums have always been in vogue; one of the most popular is P. Maudiae (above). New trends include more species, such as P. *sukhakulii* (right).

Paphiopedilum Tommie Hanes 'Val'

Paphiopedilum bellatulum 'Oceana'

Paphiopedilum sukhakulii 'Panhandle'

Paphiopedilum Farnoyo 'Stately'

green. A single flower, 3 to 4 inches across, appears on each 10 to 12-inch spike. The top sepal is whitish with dark brownish red streaks; the purple petals shade to greenish with black spots at their base; and the lip is deep purplish brown. Bloom is spring to autumn.

P. bellatulum is grown for its attractive foliage: leaves are dark green with lighter spots on the top, entirely dark purple on the underside. In summer each very short stem produces a single rounded flower, 2½ inches across, white to pale yellow with few to many dark purple spots.

P. callosum has leaves of light bluish green with darker mottling. Each 15-inch stem produces a single, long-lived flower as large as 4 inches across. The huge top sepal is white streaked with purple; the petals vary from green at the base to purple at the tip and have black spots on their upper margins. The large lip is purple brown. *P. callosum* blooms from spring to summer.

P. fairieanum is a small plant with leaves of uniform light green. In summer to early autumn, each 10-inch spike produces one flower 2½ inches across. The top sepal, white streaked and patterned with violet, has a ruffled edge. Petals also have ruffled edges; they are whitish with violet stripes. The lip is greenish violet with purple veins.

P. insigne, one of the most popular *Paphiopedilum* species, is easy to grow. Its long leaves are pale green. From autumn to spring, one or rarely two flowers appear on each 12-inch spike; the flowers are 4 to 5 inches across with a lacquered appearance. The top sepal is apple green on its center and base and white on its margin; the ruffle-edged petals are pale yellowish green with brownish purple veins; and the lip is yellowish marked with brown. Several dozen named varieties are available.

Hybrids

The paphiopedilum hybrids available today are quite different from their delicate, exotic parents: the plants are stronger, with larger and fuller flowers, and their colors are richer and better defined. Their waxy, almost lacquered, appearance is a distinctive trademark. The large, rounded top sepals represent an improvement over the species.

Popular hybrid types include the green or white "albinos," the bronzy types with spotted top sepals, and the bronzy types with top sepals in solid colors with white margins. A stunning example of the green albino type is the famous *P.* Maudiae. This hybrid is often called the beginner's orchid because it is so easy to grow.

Cypripedium

In this genus you'll find the native lady's slippers and moccasin flowers, terrestrial orchids native to the Northern Hemisphere. Appearing well above the foliage on a slender, straight stem, each flower features a pouchlike lip. All species prefer a neutral to slightly acid soil, rich in organic matter and well drained. Plant in a cool location with filtered sun. See the special feature "Conserving the Native American Orchids," page 45.

Phragmipedium

Native to Mexico and South America, *Phragmipedium* orchids are sometimes labeled *Selenipedium* or *Cypripedium*; they are commonly called mandarin orchids.

Phragmipediums prefer bright light, short of burning the foliage, and must be kept moist at all times. A fast-draining potting medium is essential. Firmly packed osmunda fiber, alone or mixed with chopped sphagnum moss, is ideal for *P. caudatum*; a mixture of chopped sphagnum moss and shredded tree fern fiber works well for other species. Fertilize phragmipediums every 2 weeks.

The long petals of *P. caudatum* make it one of the largest flowers in the orchid family. It has flower spikes to 2 feet tall, each with one to six flowers. Each flower, with its lengthy, ribbonlike petals, may reach 2½ feet long. The sepals are whitish or pale yellow with yellow green veins. The petals and lip, colored with shades of green, brown, and crimson, may be streaked and spotted. Several named varieties are available, each with slightly different colors. *P. caudatum* blooms in spring and autumn.

***Paphiopedilum* Greenhorn 'Lyda'**

Paphiopedilum Vanda M. Pearman 'Althaea'

Paphiopedilum Rose Cheek 'Ruby Doll'

...Paphiopedilum

Looking for both subtle colors and striking color combinations? This group has them. Contrast the buff pink of *P.* Vanda M. Pearman (above left) with the multihued *P.* Callo-rothschildianum (below).

Paphiopedilum Lohegnin 'Mona'

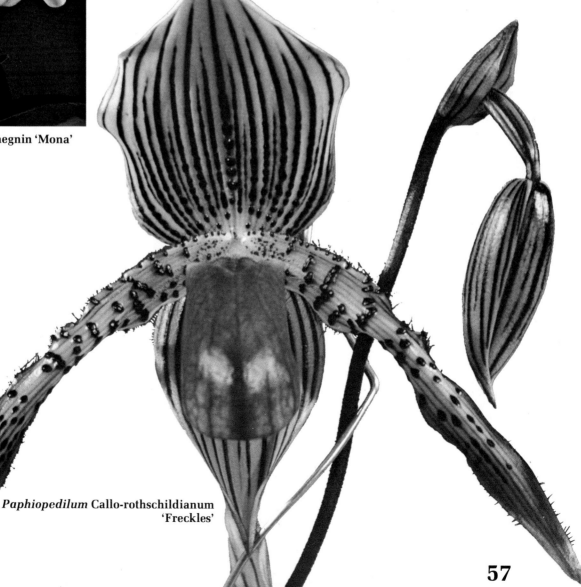

Paphiopedilum Callo-rothschildianum 'Freckles'

Popular Botanicals

"Loved only by botanists"—this was the reputation once held by the orchids known as "botanicals." But these orchids have gained new popularity. Favorites include hybrids such as *Angulocaste (Anguloa x Lycaste)*.

Maxillaria variabilis

Coelogyne bufardense

Anguloa clowesii 'Tip Toe'

Angulocaste Tudor 'Bill Zimmerman'

Bulbophyllum (Cirrhopetalum) rothschildianum 'Red Chimney'

# Botanicals

This last group of orchids includes genera that are less well known. These genera belong to a number of tribes, so the orchids in this group are not all as closely related as the members of the orchid groups listed previously. They are called botanicals because they were of little importance in early days of orchid growing, when they were appreciated only by botanists. Though some have flowers as large and handsome as orchids of the more familiar tribes, most botanicals have small flowers that are not so flamboyant. Even the small ones, however, have a delicate charm that wins them a place in many collections.

Anguloa

Members of this remarkable group of terrestrial orchids have pronounced pseudobulbs and large spoon-shaped leaves. In summer they produce dramatic tuliplike flowers. Plants prefer cool temperatures, around 50° during the night. Protect them from the summer sun or leaves will scorch, but give them some winter light. When growth has matured (generally in December or January) allow them a 4 or 5-week dry rest with occasional misting. Resume watering once bud spikes appear at the bases of the bulbs.

A. clowesii grows to 36 inches; 3-inch, brilliant yellow blooms have a creamy white lip.

Bifrenaria

These Brazilian epiphytes have large showy flowers, angled pseudobulbs, and dark green, leathery leaves. Grow under cattleya conditions (see page 32); rest plants without water for about a month after they bloom.

B. harrisoniae has 3-inch flowers that are fleshy, creamy white with a reddish purple lip. Plants grow to 18 inches tall and bloom in the spring.

Bletilla

These orchids are readily available, inexpensive, and easy to grow. Each 18 to 24-inch stem produces up to a dozen cattleya-shaped, 1 to 2-inch lavender flowers. Grassy leaves are pale green and pleated, three to six to a plant. In late winter or early spring, plant the tuberlike roots in a sandy soil where they will receive dappled sun or light shade; give plants plenty of water during spring and summer. After blooming is over in summer, let foliage ripen naturally; when the foliage begins to die back, keep plants barely moist until new growth starts in spring. Plants are hardy to about 20°; mulch them with straw in colder climates. Bletillas can be divided in early spring before growth starts, but not too often; bloom is best when plants are crowded. *Bletilla striata*, sometimes sold as *B. hyacinthina*, is the species most commonly available.

Bulbophyllum

With about 2,000 species, *Bulbophyllum* is the largest genus in the orchid family. Bulbophyllums are native to all tropical regions and most subtropical regions of the world. The curiously complex flowers featured by many species make them a delightful addition to any collection. In such a large genus—with plants so diverse in form and native habitat—cultural requirements vary widely. In fact, the preference of almost every species differs slightly from the preferences of all other species. The following guidelines are therefore quite general; a little experimentation may be required on the part of the grower.

Though intermediate temperatures (page 8) suit some bulbophyllums, most are warm growing. To avoid burning the fleshy leaves, however, provide shady conditions. Pot these orchids in tightly packed osmunda fiber, repotting infrequently. Give them abundant water while they are actively growing. Species from subtropical Asia require a 2-week dry period after growth matures, but the species listed here are tropical and do well without a rest period.

B. barbigerum features long, purple hairs on the lip that move in the slightest breeze. The 1-inch flowers are purple; the lip is green with purplish brown veins. The flowers appear in late spring and summer and have an unpleasant odor.

B. lobbii bears a single long-lived, 3 to 4-inch flower on each stem. Appearing from late spring to summer, the sweetly fragrant flowers are glossy pale yellow spotted and flushed with purple.

B. medusae is a creeping plant whose stems produce moplike clusters of many long-tailed, musty-smelling flowers. Each flower is 6 inches long (including 5-inch threadlike sepals), white to yellowish with pink or red spots. *B. medusae* blooms in autumn and winter. A similar species, *B. longissimum*, has even longer sepals.

Catasetum

These orchids have a fascinating habit: when a visiting insect steps on a unique triggering device, the catasetum flower shoots its pollen at the unsuspecting visitor. Catasetums are natives of the American tropics; most are epiphytes with large fleshy pseudobulbs and folded deciduous leaves. Easy to care for, they require a bright, well-ventilated spot and intermediate to warm temperatures (55° to 65°). Provide abundant water while they are actively growing; when leaves begin to fall, withhold water almost completely, giving just enough to keep pseudobulbs from shriveling. Resume regular watering when new growth appears in the spring. Tightly packed osmunda and tree fern fiber are recommended for potting.

C. macrocarpum is a robust, variable species; its 3½-inch, unpleasant-smelling flowers do not open fully. They are greenish with varying numbers of red dots; the lip is yellow or greenish yellow. Autumn to winter is the usual bloom time.

C. pileatum has gracefully arching 12-inch stems that produce 4-inch flowers. Appearing in autumn, the flowers are heavy-textured and fragrant, ivory to pale yellow.

Coelogyne

Containing more than 150 species, this genus is widely distributed throughout India, Malaysia, and New Guinea. These evergreen, epiphytic plants have dark green, spoon-shaped leaves that are handsome even when not in bloom. Flowers are generally small, about 1 inch across, in shades of brown, cream, beige, or green; they are produced from the youngest growth. Many species bear pendent spikes. Coelogynes prefer a shady, cool location. They require abundant water during their growing season, but excess water left standing among the leaves can cause buds to rot. Repot infrequently, and only in spring, when roots are starting.

C. cristata reaches 24 inches. Lovely large white flowers with a yellow-tinted lip bloom from winter to spring. *C. massangeana* grows to 48 inches, produces pendent stems of ochre brown flowers with a lip stained dark brown.

Cycnoches

These natives of Mexico, Central America, and South America are often called swan orchids because of the graceful curve of the lip in some species. Plants are epiphytic, with leaves and flower spikes arising from the tops of the pseudobulbs. Leaves are usually deciduous.

Place cycnoches in a brightly lighted location. After new growth is completed, plants need a definite rest period for several weeks. Flowers usually appear in summer.

C. ventricosum warscewiczii (*C. chlorochilon*) may grow to 20 inches; the 4 to 7-inch flowers are chartreuse with a white, fleshy lip.

C. egertonianum grows to 15 inches tall, with small whitish green flowers on pendent stems.

Gongora

Sometimes called Punch and Judy orchids, gongoras are colorful orchids whose native range extends from Mexico to Peru and Brazil. Intricate flowers and strongly ridged pseudobulbs are characteristic. Their long, pendulous flower stalks containing 30 to 40 flowers make gongoras popular. Grow them in hanging containers—pots or wire or slatted baskets. You can use almost any potting medium provided it drains well. Gongoras appreciate intermediate to warm temperatures (55° to 65°), mixed shade, high humidity, and moisture at almost all times. When the plants are in bud, however, give them a brief resting period by withholding water and placing them in a cooler, shadier spot.

G. quinquenervis is a variable species: the flowers may be white, brown, red, yellow, or greenish, with or without darker markings. In autumn, many fragrant 2-inch flowers bloom on spikes that may reach 2 feet or more.

Lycaste

Most of these deciduous or semideciduous orchids are epiphytic; they come from Mexico, the West Indies, and Central and South America. The long-lasting, freely-produced flowers are predominantly green, although some may be pink, white, yellow, or brown. Lycastes thrive in a cool location (50° to 55° at night, 10° warmer during the day) with good light but no direct sun. Use a fast-draining potting mixture and keep it constantly moist, except for a 2-week period after flowering; at that time, reduce water to a minimum until new growth appears.

L. aromatica grows to 16 inches; in winter short stems from the bases of new pseudobulbs bear many bright yellow, lemon-scented flowers. This species does well in a cool spot in an intermediate greenhouse (see page 8).

L. deppei may grow to 28 inches; fragrant flowers come at various times of the year. The green sepals are dotted with rich brown, the petals are white, and the lip is yellow.

L. virginalis (*L. skinneri*) reaches 30 inches and in winter produces on each stem a single 5 to 7-inch white or pink bloom, with lip spotted rose to red. Many named varieties are available. This species does not require a definite rest period.

Masdevallia

This genus of showy, tropical American orchids has characteristic lower sepals: broadened and partially joined at their bases, they are elongated into thin, pointed tail-like tips. Most of the 300 species of *Masdevallia* orchids grow in the cool, foggy heights of the Colombian Andes. These forms require cool temperatures, high humidity, abundant moisture, and a fast-draining potting medium. They also require bright light (but no direct sunlight) and good air circulation.

M. chimaera features winter flowers that range up to 9 inches long and vary in color, most commonly yellow or whitish yellow with brownish purple to blackish red markings. Several dozen color varieties are available.

M. coccinea, one of the most popular masdevallias, has sturdy, velvety flowers in a wide range of colors, from near white through oranges and reds to deep crimson purple. The form *harryana* is rich blood crimson. Bloom is late spring and summer.

M. tovarensis has bell-shaped flowers 1½ inches long; they are reddish brown inside, white with a few brown spots outside, and red brown on the tails. The bloom period extends from late spring into summer.

Maxillaria

From the tropical regions of North, Central, and South America come about 300 species of the genus *Maxillaria*. Because they are extremely variable in growth habits—ranging from creepers 2 inches high to vandalike giants reaching several feet in length—maxillarias vary in their potting requirements. The small species do well in small, fast-draining pots. Climbing forms are at their best when given some support to climb on; a tree fern fiber totem pole is good for this. Pendulous types require a slab to grow on. And the large, vandalike maxillarias will fill a trellis with their clambering stalks.

Most maxillarias grow in intermediate temperature ranges (see page 8); those listed below will grow under warm conditions also, with the exception of *M. sanderiana*, which requires cool to intermediate conditions. Diffused light suits these orchids. Provide abundant water during the growing period, but give them a 3-week dry rest period after flowering. Repot plants as soon as their potting medium begins to break down.

M. picta grows to 18 inches tall; in winter it produces heavy-textured 2½-inch flowers that may be fragrant. Flowers are tawny yellow inside, whitish spotted with reddish or purplish brown outside.

M. sanderiana has fragrant, 5 to 6-inch flowers that resemble a lycaste (see page 63) in form. They are ivory white spotted with blood red; the white lip has red and yellow markings. Summer to autumn is the bloom period.

M. tenuifolia is a popular climber that has grasslike leaves and many flower spikes on each stem. The heavy, thick flowers, 1½ to 2 inches in diameter, have a strong coconut scent. Their color varies but is usually dark red marked with yellow. Flowers appear in summer to autumn.

M. variabilis is an almost everblooming species. This plant produces small flowers that are extremely variable in color, from white or yellow marked with dark red to entirely dark red or red brown.

Pleione

These orchids are as easy to grow as ordinary spring bulb plants. Plants have angular pseudobulbs topped with a few folded leaves, usually deciduous after the flowering period. Each stem bears one 3 to 4-inch flower. Most species are hardy to about 10°, but blossoms of winter-flowering species may need protection where temperatures drop much below freezing.

After pleiones have flowered, separate the clumps of pseudobulbs and plant them in a mixture of leaf mold, chopped osmunda or sphagnum, and sand. Give them a bright spot but no direct sun. Be careful not to give them too much water until the roots are actively growing and visible growth begins. Once growth is underway, however, plants need generous amounts of water. When new pseudobulbs are mature and leaves are extended, withhold water for several weeks to encourage formation of flower buds.

Winter-flowering species include *Pleione humilis* (white to pale purple flower with yellow and violet on the lip); *P. maculata* (white and purple); and *P. praecox* (red purple). *P. formosana* (lavender purple flower with brown and yellow on the lip) blooms in spring.

Pleurothallis

Closely related to the genus *Masdevallia*, this large group of epiphytic orchids occurs throughout tropical America. The plants vary greatly in size, from the size of a thimble to several feet high. Most are decorated with small, intricate flowers. They are easy to care for, preferring light shade and constant moisture throughout the year. Temperature requirements vary from species to species: those from high elevations should be kept cool, but natives of hot, sea-level areas thrive under warm conditions. Pot pleurothallis in small containers using tightly packed osmunda or tree fern fiber, or mount them on tree fern slabs. They do not tolerate much disturbance, so repot only when absolutely necessary. As a group, *Pleurothallis* orchids are very popular among collectors, but no one species could be considered common. Check with catalogs or collectors to determine what species are available.

Sobralia

These terrestrial orchids from Central and South America bear large, showy cattleyalike flowers in summer. Plants consist of tall, reedlike stems with leaves on alternate sides for their entire length. Give sobralias a sunny location, with intermediate to warm temperatures. They require ample moisture all year, especially in early spring; decrease the amount of water, however, for a month after each year's new leafy stems are fully developed. Plants will bear flowers only when mature, and by that time they may be 5 to 6 feet tall. Plant sobralias in a potting mixture suitable for cymbidiums (see page 38) and repot infrequently.

S. leucoxantha grows to 3 feet; the 4 to 5-inch white flowers are shaded golden yellow, the throat is flushed and lined with orange. Flowering season extends from spring through summer.

S. macrantha may reach 7 feet or more; crimson purple, fragrant flowers may reach 9 inches across. Blooms appear in spring and summer.

Stanhopea

Native to Mexico, Central America, and parts of South America, the stanhopeas are epiphytes that bear large flowers in lurid color combinations. Each flower lasts only a few days. Open basket culture is necessary because flowers appear on pendent stems that frequently grow down through the potting mix and emerge through the bottom. Plants require moderate shade and copious water during growth. Give them less moisture during the rest of the year, but never let them dry out completely. Most species are quite fragrant. Stanhopeas prefer the same temperature and humidity ranges as cattleyas (see page 32).

S. wardii grows to 20 inches; its 4 to 6-inch waxy yellow, cream, or greenish white flowers are spotted with red or brown. The shape of the flowers and their carriage on pendent stems give them the look of flying birds with wings raised. Blooms appear in fall. Two similar species are S. *oculata* (yellow flowers with purple markings) and S. *tigrina* (yellow, dark red, and purple flowers).

Zygopetalum

Vividly marked, long-lasting flowers account for the popularity of this genus, composed mostly of Brazilian terrestrials. Zygopetalums have large pseudobulbs; most species have glossy foliage that becomes deciduous at maturity. Most are easily grown. Ideal conditions include a sunny exposure, intermediate to warm temperatures (55° to 65°), and good air circulation. Being terrestrial, zygopetalums require a fast-draining, highly organic potting mix: 1 part of standard potting soil mixed with 1 part of shredded osmunda, tree fern fiber, sphagnum moss, leaf mold, or fine bark (or any combination of these). Provide zygopetalums with abundant water during their growing period; allow a brief rest when the new growth matures. Feed them frequently with liberal applications of fertilizer.

Z. intermedium, the most frequently grown species, produces an erect flower spike to 2 feet high with flowers that usually open all at once. The fragrant flowers are 3 inches across; sepals and petals are of equal length. Flowers are green with reddish brown blotches; the lip is white with violet red streaks that are actually rows of colored hairs. Z. *intermedium* blooms in the winter.

Z. mackayi is a less popular but similar species that is often confused with Z. *intermedium*. Z. *mackayi* differs from the more common form in several ways: its petals are slightly shorter than its sepals, and the colored streaks are more distinct but not noticeably hairy. Z. *crinitum* is a less robust plant than the other two; it has heavier, dark streaking on the lip, covered with tiny hairs.

Gongora armeniaca

Masdevallia coccinea

Pleurothallis marmorata

Lycaste cochleata

...More Botanicals

Make your choice—the orchids known as botanicals form a diverse selection. Choose large *Sobralias* (right) or miniature *Pleurothallis* (above right). Pendulous *Gongoras* (top) contrast with upright-flowering *Lycaste* (above).

Sobralia macrantha alba x xantholeuca

Sophrocattleya Petite Fleur 'Pink Elf'

Index

Boldface numerals refer to photographs.

Photographers **American Orchid Society:** 11. **William Aplin:** 29. **William Carter:** back cover. **Beauford B. Fisher:** 2 all, 7, 8, 9, 10 all, 31 top left, center left, bottom left, bottom right, 32 all, 33 left center, 34 top right, center left, bottom, 39 top right, center left, 41 top left, top right, center right, bottom right, 42 top left, bottom right, bottom left, 47 all, 49 top right, bottom center, 50 top left, center right, bottom, 55 top left, top right, center right, bottom left, 56, 57 all, 58 center right, bottom left, bottom right, 64. **G & S Laboratory:** 19. **Bob Johnson:** 31 bottom center, 39 top left, bottom, 41 bottom left, 55 bottom right. **Hawley/Levi Orchids:** 33 top. **Lord & Burnham:** 27 left. **Ells Marugg:** 1, 13 bottom, 15 all, 16, 17, 18, 23 all, 24, 26, 28, 31 top right, 33 bottom left, bottom center, bottom right, 34 top left, top right, center right, 42 center right, 48 top, 49 top left, bottom left, bottom right, 50 top center, top right, 58 top left, top right, 63 all. **Don Normark:** 27 right. **Joe Seals:** 13 top, 40 all, 48 bottom. **Darrow M. Watt:** 4, 5 left.

Sunset Proof-of-Purchase
ISBN 0-376-03555-2